STAND OUT

Becoming the Best and the Highest

David S. Philemon

Royal Diadem Publishing Inc.

Dedication

To the Almighty God, my foundation and ever-present help. I am grateful for Your boundless love and grace that sustain me daily.
And to my mentor in ministry, Rev. George Izunwa, whose steadfast commitment to the call of God has deeply impacted my life. Your guidance and support have been invaluable, encouraging me to walk boldly in the path God has set before me. Thank you for your example and your heart for the Kingdom.

CONTENTS

ACKNOWLEDGEMENT

This book would not have been possible without the unwavering support, dedication, and talent of an extraordinary team. My deepest gratitude goes to each of you for your contributions, insights, and encouragement throughout this journey.

First and foremost, thank you to Rev. Mimi Philemon my dear wife, Rev. Shina Gentry, and and my assistant pastor Rev. Bright Amudoaghan for your incredible effort, encouragement, and belief in this project. Your support has been instrumental in bringing this vision to life.

To the dedicated leaders of Royal Diadem Publishing, Ide Imogie and Kishawna Bailey, I am immensely grateful for your belief in this project from the very beginning and for investing your time and energy into its development. Your creativity, dedication, and expertise have been the backbone of this endeavor.

I am especially grateful to the Royal Diadem Publishing team —Beulah Orogun, Emmanuella Ben-Eboh, Doyinsade Awodele, Kim Matthews, and Shante Gill, for your meticulous attention to detail, refining every page and ensuring that each word reflects our vision.

A heartfelt thank you to my family, friends, and colleagues whose unwavering support and belief in this project gave me the courage and strength to see it through.

Finally, thank you to all the readers and supporters who make this work meaningful. I am humbled and honored to share this journey with each of you.

With all my gratitude,
David Philemon

INTRODUCTION

God's Expectation for His People

As children of God, we have been called to live a life that reflects our Father's excellence. We have been created to be like Him, to think like Him, and to act like Him. Therefore, if we are going to be children of God, we might as well desire to stand out.

Desiring to stand out is not about seeking perfection or earning salvation. Rather, it is about striving for excellence in every area of our lives. It is about wanting to please God and bring glory to His name.

As Paul wrote in 2 Corinthians 13:11, "*Finally, brothers, rejoice. Aim for restoration, comfort one another, agree with one another, live in peace; and the God of love and peace will be with you*" (ESV). We are to aim for restoration, comfort one another, agree with one another, and live in peace.

If we want to do anything, we might as well want to do the highest. This means setting our sights high and striving for greatness in every area of our lives. It means being ambitious for God and wanting to achieve great things for His kingdom.

Paul wrote in Philippians 4:13, "*I can do all things through Christ who strengthens me*" (NKJV). We can do all things through Christ who strengthens us. We have the power of God living within us, and we can achieve great things when we rely on His strength.

Therefore, let us desire to stand out and strive for excellence in every area of our lives. Let us aim high and want to do our best. Let us be ambitious for God and want to achieve great things for His kingdom.

As we strive for greatness, remember that it is not about us, but God. It is not about our abilities or strengths but His power and wisdom working through us.

Let us seek to bring glory to God in all we do, and strive to be the best version of ourselves for His sake. As Paul wrote in 1 Corinthians 10:31, *"So, whether you eat or drink, or whatever you do, do all to the glory of God"* (ESV).

Do all things to the glory of God, and strive to stand out for His sake. By doing so, we will bring glory to God, and fulfill our purpose as children of God.

In the book of Genesis, we find a fascinating story about Joseph, a young man who rose from being a slave to becoming a prominent leader in Egypt. What caught God's attention was Joseph's exceptional character, diligence, and faithfulness, which ultimately led to his promotion (Genesis 39:2-4). This story points to the fact that God expects His people to rise above mediocrity and stand out by becoming the best version of themselves.

Rising in life is not just a human aspiration but God's expectation for His people. The Bible is replete with examples of individuals who achieved greatness despite their flaws and challenges because of their faith, perseverance, and determination. God hates fruitlessness, inactivity, stagnation, unproductivity, laziness, and backwardness. He desires to see His people flourish, grow, and bear fruit that reflects His greatness.

As children of God, we are expected to express the fruitfulness of God in our lives. We should constantly seek ways to improve, learn, and grow. We should strive for excellence in all aspects of our lives, whether in our relationships, careers, or spiritual walks. As the Bible says, *"And we all, who with unveiled faces contemplate the Lord's glory, are being transformed into his image with ever-increasing glory,* which comes from the Lord, who is the Spirit" (2 Corinthians 3:18).

To achieve this, we need to ask for God's wisdom, guidance, and empowerment. We must seek His mind and perspective on our lives and surrender our desires and ambitions to His will. As the Psalmist says, "*Teach me your way, Lord, that I may rely on your faithfulness; give me an undivided heart, that I may fear your name*" (Psalm 86:11).

God's Expectation for Excellence

The Bible clearly states that God expects His people to strive for excellence. In 2 Corinthians 13:11, the Apostle Paul writes, "*Finally, brothers and sisters, rejoice! Strive for full restoration, encourage one another, be of one mind, and live in peace. And the God of love and peace will be with you.*" This verse shows the importance of striving for excellence and living a life that reflects God's love and peace.

In Philippians 1:9-10, Paul prays for the believers in Philippi, saying, "*And this is my prayer: that your love may abound more and more in knowledge and depth of insight, so that you may be able to discern what is best and may be pure and blameless for the day of Christ.*" This Pauline prayer highlights the importance of continually growing and maturing in our faith and seeking to discern what is best and pleasing to God.

The Consequences of Mediocrity

On the other hand, the Bible also warns against the dangers of mediocrity and complacency. In Revelation 3:16, Jesus says, "*So, because you are lukewarm—neither hot nor cold—I am about to spit you out of my mouth.*" Here, you see the importance of being passionate and committed to our faith and avoiding a lukewarm or mediocre attitude, which is a limitation to standing out and becoming the best and the highest based on God's expectation.

In Hebrews 6:7-8, the writer warns, "*Land that drinks in the rain often falling on it and that produces a crop useful to those for whom it is farmed receives the blessing of God. But land that produces thorns and thistles is worthless and is in danger of being cursed. In the end, it will be burned."* Again, God's Word highlights the importance of being fruitful and productive in our lives and warns against the dangers of being unfruitful and unproductive.

The Path to Excellence

So, how can we strive for excellence and become the best version of ourselves? The Bible provides many principles and guidelines to help us on this journey.

Firstly, we need to have a deep and personal relationship with God. This involves spending time with Him, reading His Word, and seeking His guidance and direction.

Having a personal relationship with God is the foundation of hearing from Him and becoming the best version of ourselves. When we cultivate a deep and intimate relationship with God, we become more attuned to His voice and guidance. This relationship involves spending quality time with Him, reading His Word, and seeking His direction and wisdom.

As we nurture our relationship with God, we understand His character, love, and compassion. We start to reflect His greatness in our lives, and we desire to emulate His nature and positively impact our world. This relationship is not just about receiving blessings or favors from God; it's about loving and honoring Him with our lives.

I recall my early days of serving in the sanctuary, where I kept the place clean. Despite the distance and challenges, I prioritized being there, as it was an essential aspect of my relationship with God. This experience taught me the value of obedience, discipline, and commitment.

Moreover, my relationship with God also taught me the principle of giving. Giving is not about providing for God's needs. He has everything - **Haggai 2:8 (NKJV)** *"The silver is Mine, and the gold is Mine,' says the Lord of hosts."*

Giving expresses our love and gratitude towards Him. As I continued giving, I realized it was not just about the amount but the attitude and heart behind it. This principle has remained a vital part of my walk with God, and I continue to practice it to demonstrate my love and commitment to Him.

According to God's expectations, we must prioritize our relationship with Him to stand out and become the best and the highest:

- *Spending quality time with God, reading His Word, and seeking His guidance and direction*
- *Reflecting God's greatness in our lives by emulating His character, love, and compassion*
- *Striving to positively impact our world and leave a lasting legacy that honors God*
- *Cultivating a heart of obedience, discipline, and commitment in our service to God*
- *Practicing the principle of giving as an expression of our love and gratitude towards God*

Secondly, as we strive to stand out and become the best version of ourselves, the Bible provides us with a crucial principle: we must put off our old selves. In Ephesians 4:22-24, the Apostle Paul writes, "*You were taught, about your former way of life, to put off your old self, which is being corrupted by its deceitful desires; to be made new in the attitude of your minds; and to put on the new self, created to be like God in true righteousness and holiness.*"

Our old nature is corrupt and deceitful, and it must be put off for us to become the new creation God intends for us to be. This is not simply cleaning up or maintaining our old nature; it requires a radical transformation, a crucifixion of our old self.

I can attest to the truth of this principle in my own life. Before I came to know Christ, I had a dominant nature that drove me to defend myself at all costs. Even after being saved, this nature still lingered, and I felt the need to fight back when people mocked or rejected me.

However, as I began to walk with God and seek His guidance, I realized that this old nature did not please Him. I knew that I had to put it off, to crucify it, to become the person God wanted me to be. It wasn't easy, but with God's help, I could lay down my need for self-defense and walk in a new way, a way of humility, love, and trust.

When we put off our old self and put on the new self, we experience a radical transformation. We become a new creation, created to be like God in true righteousness and holiness. We begin to walk in a new way of love, humility, and obedience to God.

As we put off our old selves, we also begin to experience the power and freedom of living a life pleasing to God. Our old nature no longer controls us; instead, we are empowered by the Holy Spirit to live a life of excellence and righteousness.

Putting off our old self is crucial in becoming our best version and standing out. It requires a radical transformation, a crucifixion of our old nature, and a putting on of the new self. As we walk in this new way, we experience the power and freedom of living a life that is pleasing to God.

Thirdly, we need to be committed to lifelong learning and growth. This involves being open to new experiences, seeking feedback from others, and being willing to learn from our mistakes. A lifelong learner is curious, open-minded, resilient, and self- aware. They read widely, seek new experiences, ask for feedback, reflect on their experiences, and set goals and priorities for their learning.

By committing to lifelong learning, we can stay relevant, adaptable, and resilient in a rapidly changing world and achieve our full potential.

Fourthly, we need to be intentional about developing our character and integrity. This involves being honest, trustworthy, and dependable and seeking to live a life pleasing to God.

Finally, we must be willing to take risks and step out of our comfort zones. This involves being bold, courageous, and confident and seeking to impact our world positively. To become the best versions of ourselves, we must be willing to take risks and step out of our comfort zones. This involves being bold, courageous, and confident and seeking to impact our world positively.

A great example is the story of Peter walking on water, as recorded in Matthew 14:22-33. After Jesus had fed the 5,000, He instructed His disciples to get into a boat and cross the lake while He dismissed the crowd. As the disciples sailed, a strong wind arose, and the waves tossed about the boat. Meanwhile, Jesus came to them, walking on the water. When Peter saw Jesus, he asked Him to command him to come to Him on the water.

Jesus replied, "*Come*," and Peter stepped out of the boat and began to walk on the water towards Jesus. However, when he saw the strong wind and the waves, he became afraid and began to sink. Jesus immediately reached out and caught him, saying, "*You of little faith, why did you doubt?*" Peter's willingness to take a risk and step out of his comfort zone ultimately led to a remarkable experience of walking on water with Jesus.

Peter's experience teaches us several valuable lessons. Peter could have stayed in the boat and played it safe, but he chose to take a risk and step out in faith. Don't stay in the boat of mediocrity; step out of the boat and do the impossible. Peter trusted that Jesus would enable him to walk on the water and took a step of faith. Take a bold step of faith – trusting God's helping hand, and He will help you become the best version of yourself. When Peter became afraid, he began to sink. We must overcome our fears and doubts and trust God's power and presence.

By applying these lessons to our lives, we can develop the courage and confidence to step out of our comfort zones and become the best and highest.

Standing out and becoming the best version of ourselves is a lifelong journey that requires commitment, dedication, and perseverance. It involves striving for excellence, seeking to live a life that is pleasing to God, and being intentional about developing our character and integrity.

This book, "Stand Out: Becoming the Best and the Highest," will tell us what it means to become the best versions of ourselves and to soar above mediocrity. We will look at the biblical ideals and ideas supporting a successful life and offer helpful advice for doing so. This book is for everyone, whether you're a Christian trying to grow in your faith or someone trying to better your life and reach your objectives. Let's go on this adventure to learn what it means to be our greatest and most ideal version.

CHAPTER ONE

God's Servant: Displaying His Splendor

"He said to me, 'You are my servant, Israel, in whom I will display my splendor.' But I said, 'I have labored in vain; I have spent my strength for nothing at all. Yet what is due me is in the Lord's hand, and my reward is with my God.' And now the Lord says— he who formed me in the womb to be his servant to bring Jacob back to him and gather Israel to himself, for I am honored in the eyes of the Lord and my God has been my strength— he says: 'It is too small a thing for you to be my servant to restore the tribes of Jacob and bring back those of Israel I have kept. I will also make you a light for the Gentiles, that my salvation may reach to the ends of the earth." **Isaiah 49:3-6 NIV**

Have you ever felt your efforts are in vain and you're not progressing? You're not alone. Isaiah, the prophet, felt this way too. In Isaiah 49:3b (NLT), he replied to the Lord, "...but my work seems so useless! I have spent my strength for nothing and to no purpose..." Despite his inadequacy, God reassured Isaiah that He would use him to display His splendor. As Isaiah 49:4c (NLT) says, "...*Yet what is due me is in the Lord's hand, and my reward is with my God.*"

This promise is not just limited to Isaiah; it's available to everyone willing to trust God and leave their lives in His hands. As God's servants, we are called to display His splendor and manifest His greatness in our lives. But what does it mean to be a servant of God?

The term "servant" is frequently applied to those who performed some service, task, or mission for the Lord. In the

Bible, God's servants are people called or chosen to stand out, to display His glory, and to manifest God's greatness in life. They are individuals who have dedicated their lives to serving God and fulfilling His purposes.

As God's servants, we are not defined by our past mistakes or failures. God doesn't look at our weaknesses or shortcomings to determine our worth or potential.

Instead, He picks out the best from the dirt, just as He did with the Israelites, who were enslaved people in Egypt. Exodus 19:5 (NIV) says, "*Now if you obey me fully and keep my covenant, then out of all nations, you will be my treasured possession.*"

God's servants are not limited by their circumstances or background. They are individuals called and chosen by God to fulfill a specific purpose or mission and to stand out. As 1 Corinthians 1:27-28 (NIV) says, "*But God chose the foolish things of the world to shame the wise; God chose the weak things of the world to shame the strong. God chose the lowly things of this world and the despised things—and the things that are not— to nullify the things that are.*"

As God's servants, we are called to trust Him completely, leaving our lives and future in His hands. We must believe that He can do exceeding abundantly above all that we ask or think, according to the power that works in us (Ephesians 3:20). We must have faith that He will use us to display His splendor despite our weaknesses or shortcomings.

In Isaiah 49:3-6, God reassures Isaiah that He will use him to display His splendor despite his feelings of inadequacy. God tells Isaiah that He will make him a light to the Gentiles and that His salvation will reach the ends of the earth. This promise is not just limited to Isaiah; it's available to everyone willing to trust God and leave their lives in His hands.

As we embark on this journey of becoming God's servants, remember that our past mistakes or failures do not define us, nor are we limited by our circumstances or background. Instead, we are called to trust God completely, leaving our lives and future in His hands. According to the power that works in us, we must believe He can do exceedingly above all we ask or think.

As we trust God and obey His commands, we will begin to experience the fulfillment of His promise to make us a light to the Gentiles and to use us to display His splendor. We will become the best version of ourselves and fulfill the purpose for which God created us.

This chapter will explore what it means to be a servant of God and how we can fulfill our role by standing out as His servants. We will examine the characteristics of a servant of God and how we can develop these characteristics in our own lives.

However, before I proceed, I must let you know that God is saying to you reading this book now, "You are My servant." It doesn't matter how your life may look today; you are God's servant. You are not Satan's servant; you are not a servant to evil powers; you are not a servant to witches and wizards. You can pause momentarily and scream, "I am God's servant for the rest of my life."

The Characteristics of a Servant of God

As we explore what it means to be a servant of God, let's examine the characteristics that define a true servant of God. In Matthew 20:26-28 (NIV), Jesus says, "Whoever wants to become great among you must be your servant, and whoever wants to be first must be your slave—just as the Son of Man did not come to be served, but to serve, and to give his life as a ransom for many."

A true servant of God is characterized by humility, obedience, and a willingness to serve others. They are not motivated by a desire for power, wealth, or recognition but by a desire to please God and fulfill His purposes.

Humility: The Foundation of Servanthood

Humility is the foundation of servanthood. It involves

recognizing our limitations and weaknesses and being willing to learn from others. In 1 Peter 5:5-6 (NIV), we are instructed to "*clothe yourselves with humility toward one another, because, 'God opposes the proud but shows favor to the humble.' Humble yourselves, therefore, under God's mighty hand, that he may lift you up in due time.*"

As servants of God, we must cultivate humility in our lives. This involves recognizing our dependence on God and our need for His guidance and strength. It also involves being willing to listen to others, learn from them, and receive correction. I'll never forget the correction I received from my biological father.

The Importance of Humility in Servanthood

As servants of God, we are expected to display the characteristics of our leader, Jesus Christ. One of the most essential characteristics of Christ is *humility*. In Philippians 2:5-8 (NLT), we are instructed to "*have the same mindset as Christ Jesus: Who, being in very nature God, did not consider equality with God something to be used to his advantage; rather, he made himself nothing by taking the very nature of a servant, being made in human likeness. And being found in appearance as a man, he humbled himself by becoming obedient to death—even death on a cross!*"

Humility is essential in servanthood because it allows us to put others before ourselves and serve them with a willing heart. When we are humble, we recognize our limitations and weaknesses and seek help and guidance from others. We also receive correction and feedback from others and learn from our mistakes.

My own experience has taught me the importance of humility in servanthood. Growing up, my biological father, a very disciplined man, taught me how to serve God in His vineyard with all humility. He instructed me never to refuse to serve in the sanctuary, even if others refused. He told me that refusing to serve because others refused was a sign of pride, not humility.

A humble servant of God does not look to others for validation or recognition. Instead, they follow the example of Jesus Christ, who humbled Himself and became obedient to death on the cross. Philippians 2:9-11 (NLT) says, *"Therefore God exalted him to the highest place and gave him the name that is above every name, that at the name of Jesus, every knee should bow, in heaven and on earth and under the earth, and every tongue acknowledge that Jesus Christ is Lord, to the glory of God the Father."*

Humility is a crucial characteristic of a servant of God, essential for becoming the best and highest version of ourselves. When we humble ourselves and serve others with a willing heart, we demonstrate our commitment to following the example of Jesus
Christ. We also open ourselves to receiving God's blessings and favor and experiencing the joy and fulfillment of serving others.

Now, let's examine the importance of obedience in servanthood and how it can help us become the best and highest version of ourselves.

Obedience: The Key to Fulfilling God's Purposes

Obedience is the key to fulfilling God's purposes in our lives. As servants of God, we are called to obey His commands and follow His instructions. In John 14:15 (NIV), Jesus says, *"If you love me, keep my commands."*

Obedience involves trusting God and His ways, even when we don't understand them. It involves stepping out of our comfort zones to fulfill God's purposes. As servants of God, we must cultivate obedience, recognizing that it is the key to fulfilling God's plans and purposes.

As servants of God who want to display His splendor, we must obey God's instructions. Obedience is the key to fulfilling

God's purposes in our lives. In 1 John 5:3 (NIV), we are told that *"this is love for God: to keep his commands. And his commands are not burdensome."*

God's instructions are not grievous or burdensome. Instead, they are designed to guide us and help us fulfill our life purpose. However, obedience to God's instructions requires discipline, commitment, and a willingness to trust God and His ways.

A great example of obedience in the Bible is the story of Abraham. In Genesis 12:1-4 (NIV), God instructed Abraham to leave his country, his people, and his father's household and go to the land God would show him. Abraham obeyed God's instructions, even though it meant leaving behind everything familiar to him.

As a result of his obedience, Abraham became the father of many nations, and his descendants became numerous and influential people. In Romans 4:18-22 (NIV), we are told that Abraham's faith was credited to him as righteousness and that he is the father of all who believe.

My experience has taught me the importance of obedience in fulfilling God's purposes. In 1995 and 1996, I followed and obeyed all the instructions given to me by the Lord. These instructions included attending all services in the church denomination where I belonged, keeping up with all my financial obligations, and serving as a sanctuary keeper.

I obeyed these instructions, not because I felt like it, but because I wanted to please God and fulfill His purposes. And I can boldly say that it paid off. I am becoming the best and the highest version of myself and fulfilling my purpose in life.

Obedience to God's instructions doesn't exclude anything written in His Word. We must be careful not to pick and choose which instructions we want to obey; instead, we must abide by God's commands, no matter how difficult or challenging they seem.

In 2 Timothy 3:16-17 (NIV), we are told that "*all Scripture is God-breathed and is useful for teaching, rebuking, correcting and training in righteousness, so that the servant of God may be thoroughly equipped for every good work.*"

God's Word is yes and amen, and we must obey it, no matter what. We must not be misled by false teachings or interpretations of God's Word. Instead, we must study God's Word for ourselves and obey its instructions, no matter how difficult or challenging they may seem.

Dedication and Commitment: Essential Characteristics of God's Servants

Dedication and commitment are essential qualities that enable us to become our best and highest version. In our walk with God, dedication and commitment are crucial in displaying God's splendor and fulfilling our purpose in life.

Dedication involves being entirely devoted to God and His kingdom business. It requires us to prioritize our relationship with God above all else and to be willing to make sacrifices to serve Him. In 1 Corinthians 3:5-7 (NIV), we are told, "*What, after all, is Apollos? And what is Paul? Only servants, through whom you came to believe—as the Lord has assigned to each his task. I planted the seed, Apollos watered it, but God has been making it grow.*"

On the other hand, commitment involves being faithful and loyal to God and His kingdom business. It requires us to persevere in our service to God, even when faced with challenges and obstacles. In 2 Timothy 2:3-4 (NIV), we are instructed to "*endure hardship with us like a good soldier of Christ Jesus. No one serving as a soldier gets entangled in civilian affairs but rather tries to please his commanding officer.*"

My experience has taught me the importance of dedication and commitment to serving God. In my early years of walking with God, I amazed my peers with my commitment to my church lineage, which God had shown me and instructed me to join. My biological father played a significant role in teaching me the value of dedication. He often told me, "If you run away from being part of the school's sanitation work like other students do, who will do the work?" He would send me back to complete my tasks, and this became a principle for me to stay dedicated and committed.

I brought this principle into my dedication and commitment to the kingdom business. I was so dedicated and committed that I often walked to the church premises for two
hours to clean and wash the chairs and attend other weekly services. I attended services four times weekly, and if I didn't have to join a bus that took forty-five minutes to get to the destination, I would have to walk.

God's servant must be dedicated and committed to kingdom business to become the best and the highest. Dedication and commitment require us to prioritize our relationship with God, persevere in our service to Him, and make sacrifices to fulfill our purpose in life. By dedicating ourselves to God's kingdom business, we will experience the fulfillment of God's promise to make us the best and the highest. We will become more like Christ, demonstrating His humility, obedience, and willingness to serve others.

Dedication and commitment are essential characteristics of God's servants. They enable us to become the best and highest version of ourselves and to display God's splendor in our lives. As we prioritize our relationship with God, persevere in our service to Him, and make sacrifices to fulfill our purpose in life, we will experience the fulfillment of God's promise to make us the best and highest.

Displaying God's Splendor: Becoming the Best and Highest

In Isaiah 60:19 (NIV), we are told, "*The sun will no more be your light by day, nor will the brightness of the moon shine on you, for the Lord will be your everlasting light, and your God will be your glory.*" As God's servants, we are called to display God's splendor. This requires us to cultivate the abovementioned characteristics to reflect God's glory and majesty.

One of the essential characteristics of a servant of God mentioned is humility. When we humble ourselves before God, we recognize our limitations and weaknesses and become more dependent on Him. This humility enables us to receive God's guidance and direction and fulfill our life purpose.

Obedience is another crucial characteristic of a servant of God mentioned above. When we obey God's instructions, we demonstrate our love and commitment to Him. Obedience requires us to trust God and His ways, even when we don't understand them. It also requires us to be willing to make sacrifices to fulfill God's purposes.

Dedication and commitment are also necessary characteristics of a servant of God. When we are dedicated and committed to God's kingdom business, we prioritize our relationship with God above all else, and we persevere in our service to Him, even when faced with challenges and obstacles.

As we cultivate these characteristics in our lives, we will begin to experience the fulfillment of God's promise to make us the best and highest. We will become more like Christ, demonstrating His humility, obedience, and willingness to serve others.

We will also experience the joy and fulfillment that comes from serving God and fulfilling our purpose in life.

In Isaiah 60:19 (NIV), we are told that God will be our everlasting light, and our God will be our glory. When we display God's splendor, we reflect His glory and majesty to the world. We become a light in the darkness, shining brightly for all to see.

Displaying God's Splendor: Separating Ourselves from Contamination and Corruption

As God's servants, we are called to display His splendor and to become the best and highest version of ourselves. However, to achieve this, we must first understand that God knows those who are His, and we must run away from evil.

"But God's firm foundation stands, bearing this seal (inscription): 'The Lord knows those who are His,' and, 'Let everyone who names [himself by] the name of the Lord depart from wickedness and iniquity.' But in a great house, there are not only vessels of gold and silver but also of wood and clay. Some are for honorable and noble use [as vessels of gold and silver], while others are for menial and ignoble use [as vessels of wood and clay]. So whoever cleanses himself [from what is ignoble and unclean, who separates himself from contact with contaminating and corrupting influences] will [then himself] be a vessel set apart and useful for the Master's use, prepared for every good work." **2 Timothy 2:19-22 (AMPC)**

This passage explains that we must separate ourselves from contaminating and corrupting influences as God's servants. We must be special utensils for honorable use, ready for the Master to use to display His splendor. When we separate ourselves from contamination and corruption, we will be useful in God's hand in manifesting His splendor.

We must also understand that God cannot see that we have separated ourselves from contaminating and corrupting influences and then He abandons us as His servants. Instead, He will use us to display His splendor, and we will shine forth in all areas. As the passage says, *"God never abandons willing and ready vessels."*

Nobody can steal our real glory as God's servants. In Esther 6:1-14 (NKJV), we read the story of Mordecai, a faithful servant of God. Haman, a wicked and corrupt man, only briefly stole Mordecai's glory. God took it back and restored it to Mordecai, and the glory was evident for all to see.

The passage says, *"So the king's scribes were called at that time, in the third month (that is, the month of Sivan), on the twenty-third day; and it was written, according to all that Mordecai commanded, to the Jews, the satraps, the governors, and the princes*

of the provinces which are from India to Ethiopia, one hundred and twenty-seven
provinces, to every province in its own script, to every people in their own language, and the Jews in their own script and language. And he wrote in the name of King Ahasuerus, sealed it with the king's signet ring, and sent letters by couriers on horseback, riding on royal horses bred from swift steeds."

Haman could not sustain what he stole from Mordecai. Instead, God restored Mordecai's glory and exalted him in the kingdom. As God's servants, we must understand that our glory and splendor come from God, and nobody can steal it from us.

As God's servants, we must separate ourselves from contaminating and corrupting influences to display God's splendor. We must be special utensils for honorable use, ready for the Master to use to display His splendor. When we separate ourselves from contamination and corruption, we will be useful in God's hand in manifesting His splendor. We will shine forth in all areas, and our glory and splendor will be evident for all to see.

Honorable, Noble, and Profitable Purposes: God's Desire for His Servants

As children of God, we are called to live lives that honor and glorify Him. God wants to use us for honorable, noble, and profitable purposes, but we must first make ourselves available for these purposes.

Before we proceed, let us pause for a while and pray:

"God, I dedicate my life to you, my ministry, career, business, body. I ask that you use me for honorable, noble, and profitable purposes. Help me to make myself available for your use and to live a life that honors and glorifies you."

Let us now look into what it means to make ourselves available for God's honorable, noble, and profitable purposes.

We must surrender our lives to Him to make ourselves available for God's purposes. This means letting go of our desires, ambitions, and plans instead of seeking God's will and purpose for our lives.

In Romans 12:1-2 (NIV), we are instructed to "*offer your bodies as a living sacrifice, holy and pleasing to God—which is your true and proper worship. Do not conform to the pattern of this world, but be transformed by the renewing of your mind. Then you will be able to test and approve what God's will is—his good, pleasing, and perfect will.*"

We must also be willing to be molded and shaped by God into the vessels He desires us to be. This means being open to God's correction, guidance, and instruction and willing to learn and grow in our faith.

In Jeremiah 18:1-6 (NIV), we read the potter and clay story. The potter can shape and mold the clay into the vessel He desires, but the clay must be willing to be shaped and molded. Similarly, we must be willing to be shaped and molded by God into the vessels He desires us to be.

Furthermore, we must be willing to serve God with our whole hearts, souls, minds, and strength. This means committing to God's kingdom business and sacrificing to fulfill God's purposes.

In Mark 12:30 (NIV), Jesus instructs us to "*love the Lord your God with all your heart, with all your soul, with all your mind and with all your strength.*"

Finally, we must be willing to trust God and His ways, even when we don't understand them. This means having faith in God's sovereignty and providence, being willing to wait on Him, and trusting in His timing.

In Proverbs 3:5-6 (NIV), we are instructed to "*trust in the Lord with all your heart and lean not on your own understanding; in all your ways submit to him, and he will make your paths straight.*"

God wants to use us for honorable, noble, and profitable purposes, but we must first make ourselves available for these purposes. This means surrendering our lives to God, being willing to be molded and shaped by Him, serving God with our whole heart, soul, mind, and strength, and trusting God and His ways. As we make ourselves available for God's purposes, we will fulfill our purpose in life.

Trails and Testing of God's Servant:
Becoming the Best and Highest

As God's servants, we are called to walk with God and fulfill our purpose in life. However, this journey is not without its challenges and obstacles. In Proverbs 17:1-3,6 (TPT, MSG), we are told that the testing of God is not meant to make us losers but to make us reliable. God wants us to be trustworthy men and women who can be trusted to fulfill our purpose in life.

The trials and testing of God's servants are designed to refine us and make us more like Christ. They are meant to help us develop the characteristics of a servant of God, such as humility, obedience, dedication, and commitment. As we go through these trials and tests, we must remember that God is always in our business and working to make us the best and highest version of ourselves.

Some people do not care about durability and legacy, and God fails to regard them. However, as God's servants, we must be concerned about the legacy we leave behind, our impact on others, and how we represent God to the world.

If God invests in us, it matters to Him who we keep as friends, acquaintances, and life partners. We must be careful about the company we keep and surround ourselves with people who will help us fulfill our purpose in life.

There are certain people God doesn't bother Himself with, but there are others with whom, if they make an inevitable move, God is always in their business. Knowing that God is always in our business is joyful because He constantly works to make us the best and highest version of ourselves.

As we walk with God, we must expect trials and testing. If we are not experiencing any tests or trials, it may be because we have passed all the tests, and God is giving us a little break. Alternatively, it may be because we have failed all the tests and have been demoted. Or, it may be because God is preparing us for more complex tests.

Wherever we are today may be suitable for our level, but we must not blame God if we haven't seen the desired changes. Instead, we must ask God, "What am I missing?" We must be willing to learn and grow and to make the necessary changes to fulfill our purpose in life.

As God's servants, we must understand that being a child of God is not just a matter of biological connection but also of spiritual connection. We must be willing to implement principles and multiply our inheritance. We must be willing to pay the price to be served and recognize the Father's wisdom.

The trials and testing of God's servants are designed to refine us and make us more like Christ. They are meant to help us develop the characteristics of a servant of God, such as humility, obedience, dedication, and commitment. As we go through these trials and tests, we must remember that God is always in our business and working to make us the best and highest version of ourselves.

CHAPTER TWO

From Bruised to Blessed: How Jesus' Sacrifice Empowers Us to Become the Best and Highest

"But He was wounded for our transgressions, He was bruised for our iniquities; The chastisement for our peace was upon Him, And by His stripes we are healed."

"Yet it pleased the Lord to bruise Him; He has put Him to grief. When You make His soul an offering for sin, He shall see His seed, He shall prolong His days, And the pleasure of the Lord shall prosper in His hand." Isaiah 53:5, 10 (NKJV)

The Disfiguration of Jesus and the Configuration of Humanity

In Isaiah 53, the Bible describes the disfiguration of Jesus, who was bruised and wounded for our transgressions. This passage is loaded with a powerful reminder of the sacrifice Jesus made on our behalf, and how His disfiguration led to our configuration.

As the passage states, *"He was despised and rejected by men, a man of sorrows and acquainted with grief; and as one from whom men hide their faces he was despised, and we esteemed him not"* (Isaiah 53:3, ESV). Jesus was despised and rejected by men, and He was wounded for our transgressions.

But despite His disfiguration, Jesus' sacrifice led to our configuration. As the passage states, *"But he was wounded for our transgressions; he was crushed for our iniquities; upon him was the chastisement that brought us peace, and with his stripes we are healed*" (Isaiah 53:5, ESV). Jesus' wounds brought us peace, and His stripes healed us.

This is an awesome illustration of the love and sacrifice of Jesus. We are told in the scriptures that, "*All we like sheep have gone astray; we have turned—everyone—to his own way; and the Lord has laid on him the iniquity of us all*" (Isaiah 53:6, ESV). We have all gone astray, but Jesus took our iniquity upon Himself.

God is an awesome God, who knew that our disfiguration would never lead to His glorification. But He also knew that He could damage Himself for us and then rebuild Himself. This is the work of the Shepherd, who lays down His life for the sheep.

As simple as what the Good Shepherd can do for His sheep, "*He was oppressed, and he was afflicted, yet he opened not his mouth; like a lamb that is led to the slaughter, and like a sheep that before its shearers is silent, so he opened not his mouth*" (Isaiah 53:7, ESV). Jesus was oppressed and afflicted, but He did not open His mouth. He was like a lamb led to the slaughter, silent before His shearers.

What a powerful reminder of the sacrifice that Jesus made on our behalf. He was wounded for our transgressions, and His stripes healed us. He was oppressed and afflicted, but He did not open His mouth.

The Redemption of Humanity

Redemption is the act of buying back something that has been lost or sold. In the case of humanity, we were lost due to sin, and we were sold into slavery to the devil. But Jesus came to redeem us, to buy us back from the slave market of sin.

"But he was wounded for our transgressions; he was crushed for our iniquities; upon him was the chastisement that brought us peace, and with his stripes we are healed" (Isaiah 53:5, ESV). Jesus was wounded for our transgressions, and His stripes healed us. Yes, it did!

This is the power of redemption. Jesus came to redeem us, to buy us back from the slave market of sin. I want you to reflect on the redemption of humanity, and remember the love and sacrifice of Jesus and He was wounded for our transgressions, and that His stripes healed us.

Redemption is not just about being saved from sin; it is also about being restored to our rightful place as children of God. *"But now, thus says the Lord, your Creator, O Jacob, and He who formed you, O Israel: 'Fear not, for I have redeemed you; I have called you by name; you are Mine'"* (Isaiah 43:1, NKJV). That's the assurance we have.

We are redeemed, and we are called by name. We are God's children, and we are restored to our rightful place as heirs. As it is written in Romans 8:14-17, *"For all who are led by the Spirit of God are sons of God. For you did not receive the spirit of slavery to fall back into fear, but you have received the Spirit of adoption as sons, by whom we cry, 'Abba! Father!' The Spirit himself bears witness with our spirit that we are children of God, and if children, then heirs—heirs of God and fellow heirs with Christ"* (ESV).

We are children of God, and we are heirs of God's kingdom. The blood of Jesus has redeemed us, and we have been restored to our rightful place as children of God.

The Power of Redemption

Redemption is the power that sets us free from the bondage of sin. It is the power that restores us to our rightful place as children of God. It is the power that gives us the authority to become children of God.

As John wrote in 1 John 3:1-3, *"See what kind of love the Father has given to us, that we should be called children of God; and so we are. The reason why the world does not know us is that it did not know him. Beloved, we are God's children now, and what we will be has not yet appeared; but we know that when he appears we shall be like him because we shall see him as he is"* (ESV).

We are God's children, and we have been redeemed by the

blood of Jesus. We have been restored to our rightful place as children of God, and we have been given the authority to become children of God.

I want you to consider the words of Paul in Romans 8:18, "*For I consider that the sufferings of this present time are not worth comparing with the glory that is to be revealed to us*" (ESV). The glory that is to be revealed to us is far greater than any suffering we may endure in this present time. Let us look forward to that glory, and let us strive to live our lives by our newfound identity as children of God.

Empowered by His Sacrifice

The Bible contains several stories of bruised, rejected, and despised individuals who ultimately became blessed and highly esteemed. One such character is Joseph, the son of Jacob. Joseph's story teaches us that God constantly works to achieve a greater good despite suffering and rejection.

Joseph was a young man with a bright future ahead of him. However, his brothers, fueled by jealousy and resentment, conspired against him and sold him into slavery. Joseph was taken to Egypt, where he was forced to serve as a slave in the household of Potiphar, a high-ranking official in Pharaoh's court.

Despite his difficult circumstances, Joseph remained faithful to God and trusted His sovereignty. As a result, God blessed Joseph and gave him success in everything he did. Joseph's master, Potiphar, took notice of his exceptional abilities and promoted him to oversee his entire household.

However, Joseph's success was short-lived. Potiphar's wife, driven by lust and deceit, falsely accused Joseph of attempting to seduce her. As a result, Joseph was thrown into prison, where he languished for many years.

Despite his unjust imprisonment, Joseph trusted God's ability to make him the best and the highest. He had a confident attitude toward God and believed He would realize his dreams. God was working behind the scenes to bring about Joseph's deliverance in His infinite wisdom and mercy. That same God is working behind the scenes for you today. Amen!

Years later, Pharaoh had a dream that no one could interpret. The cupbearer, who had been imprisoned with Joseph, remembered Joseph's exceptional ability to interpret dreams. He told Pharaoh about Joseph, and Pharaoh sent for him. Joseph interpreted Pharaoh's dream, and his wisdom and insight impressed Pharaoh so much that he appointed Joseph as his second-in-command over all of Egypt. Joseph's brothers, who had sold him into slavery years earlier, came to Egypt seeking food during a famine. In a dramatic turn of events, Joseph revealed his true identity to his brothers and forgave them for their past transgressions.

The story of Joseph is a message to us all that even while suffering and rejection, God is always working to bring about a greater good. Joseph was bruised, rejected, and despised by his brothers, but ultimately, he became blessed and highly esteemed by Pharaoh and the entire nation of Egypt.

In Isaiah 53:5, we read, *"But He was wounded for our transgressions, He was bruised for our iniquities; The chastisement for our peace was upon Him, and by His stripes, we are healed."* Jesus, like Joseph, was bruised and wounded for our sake. He suffered and died on the cross to pay the penalty for our sins and to bring us healing and restoration.

In Isaiah 53:10, we read, *"Yet it pleased the Lord to bruise Him; He has put Him to grief. When You make His soul an offering for sin, He shall see His seed, He shall prolong His days, And the pleasure of the Lord shall prosper in His hand."* Jesus' sacrifice on the cross was not in vain. Jesus brought us salvation, healing, and restoration through His death and resurrection.

As we reflect on Joseph's story and Jesus's sacrifice on the cross, we understand the power of transformation available to us. We can move from being bruised and rejected to being blessed and highly esteemed. We can experience the healing and restoration that Jesus brings and fulfill our purpose in life.

This chapter will explore how Jesus' sacrifice on the cross empowers us to become our best and highest version. We will examine the characteristics of a servant of God and how these characteristics are developed through our experiences and challenges. We will also discuss how Jesus' sacrifice on the cross gives us the power to overcome sin and to live a life that honors and glorifies God.

Unlocking the Power of Jesus' Sacrifice

The sacrifice of Jesus on the cross is a pivotal moment in human history. Isaiah 53:1-10 (MSG) vividly depicts the scene, using imagery that conveys the depth of Jesus' suffering. The gold bar, bees, doors, stinging, and death are excellent reminders of the price Jesus paid for our salvation.

But Jesus' sacrifice was not just about saving us from our sins but empowering us to live a life that honors and glorifies God. He wants us to be vessels of honor, noble, and profitable, called to be the best and the highest.

The purpose of Jesus' sacrifice goes beyond just dying for our sins. He saved us so that He could be glorified through us. He wants to manifest Himself in others through us. This means we are called to be ambassadors of Christ, representing God's kingdom on earth and bringing glory to His name.

As we reflect on Jesus' sacrifice, we must remember that He did not just die for our sins; He also rose from the dead, defeating death and giving us the power to overcome sin and death. This means we do not have to be held back by past mistakes or current circumstances. We can live a life empowered by the Holy Spirit that glorifies God and fulfills our purpose.

In 1 Corinthians 2:6-9 (TPT), we read: "*We do, however, speak a message of wisdom among the mature, but not the wisdom of this age or of the rulers of this age, who are coming to nothing. No, we declare God's wisdom, a mystery that has been hidden and that God destined for our glory before time began. None of the rulers of this age understood it, for if they had, they would not have crucified the Lord of glory."*

This passage reminds us that Jesus' sacrifice was not just about saving us from our sins but about revealing God's wisdom to us. This wisdom is not the wisdom of this age but rather a mystery that has been hidden and destined for our glory.

As we move forward, remember that we are not just ordinary people. We are children of God, called to be ambassadors of Christ. We are called to represent God's kingdom on earth and bring glory to His name. Let us live purposefully and intentionally, refusing to settle for an ordinary life. Instead, let us insist on being the best and the highest, bringing glory to God, and fulfilling our purpose in life.

Jesus' sacrifice on the cross was not just about saving us from our sins but empowering us to live a life that honors and glorifies God. He wants us to be vessels of honor, noble, and profitable, called to be the best and the highest. Remember that we are not just ordinary people but children of God, called to be ambassadors of Christ. Let us live purposefully and intentionally, refusing to settle for an ordinary life. Instead, let us insist on being the best and the highest, bringing glory to God, and fulfilling our purpose in life.

Quantifying the Value of Christ's Sacrifice

As believers, we often find ourselves stuck in a rut, unable to move beyond our current circumstances. We may feel like we're not living up to our full potential and may not know why. According to the Bible, many believers don't go beyond what they're worth because they cannot quantify the worth of Christ's sacrifice on the cross.

In other words, we don't understand the actual value of what Jesus did for us. We don't grasp the depth of His love and the extent of His sacrifice. As a result, we settle for a mediocre life, one that is far below what God has called us to.

This lack of understanding is evident in our lives. Instead of channeling our energies towards advancing the Kingdom of God, we often fight each other in the church. We spend more time arguing with our brothers and sisters in Christ than praying for them and working together to build the Kingdom.

We also waste a lot of energy on social media, attacking each other and demeaning the work of different denominations. The energy we use to criticize and tear each other down could be used for something much better. We could use that energy to pray for each other, support each other, and work together to advance the Kingdom.

But instead, we often find ourselves stuck in a cycle of negativity and criticism. We forget that we are all part of the same body and are all called to work together to build the Kingdom.

So, the question is, since Jesus Christ came into your life, has He marked your life and said that the sacrifice He paid is worth it? What has He looked at you and said? Can you quantify the worth of His death in your life?

Jesus wants to look at you and be glad that the price He paid for you is worth it. He wants to see that you understand the value of His sacrifice and live a life that reflects that understanding.

As the Bible says in 1 Corinthians 6:20 (NIV), *"You were bought at a price. Therefore, honor God with your bodies."* We were bought at a price that Jesus Christ paid on the cross. And because of that, we are called to honor God with our lives.

But how can we do that if we don't understand the actual value of Christ's sacrifice? How can we honor God with our lives if we don't grasp the depth of His love and the extent of His sacrifice?

The answer is we can't. We will continue to live mediocre lives, lives that are far below what God has called us to. We will continue to waste our energy on petty squabbles and criticisms rather than using that energy to build the

Kingdom.

But it doesn't have to be that way. We can quantify the worth of Christ's sacrifice in our lives, understand the true value of what Jesus did for us, and live our lives in a way that reflects that understanding.

As the Bible says in Philippians 1:20 (NIV), *"I eagerly expect and hope that I will in no way be ashamed, but will have sufficient courage so that now as always Christ will be exalted in my body, whether by life or death."*
Paul desired to live a life that exalted Christ, whether by life or death. He wanted to ensure that he honored God and reflected the true value of Christ's sacrifice.

And that's what God wants from us as well. He wants us to live lives that honor Him and reflect the actual value of Christ's sacrifice. He wants us to understand that we were bought at a price and to live our lives in a way that reflects that understanding.

So, let's choose today to quantify the worth of Christ's sacrifice in our lives. Let's understand the value of what Jesus did for us and live our lives in a way that reflects that understanding.

Let's ask ourselves, whose life is improving because of me? Am I using my energy to build the Kingdom, or am I wasting it on petty squabbles and criticisms?

Let's choose to be vessels of honor, noble, and profitable. Let's live lives that exalt Christ, whether by life or death. Let's understand the value of Christ's sacrifice and live our lives to reflect that understanding.

As the Bible says in 2 Corinthians 5:15 (NIV), *"And he died for all, that those who live should no longer live for themselves but for him who died for them and was raised again."*

Jesus died for us so that we could live for Him. He wants us to understand the value of His sacrifice and live our lives in a way that reflects that understanding.

When we truly grasp the depth of Christ's love and the extent of His sacrifice, we will be motivated to live our lives in a way that honors Him. We will want to use our energy and resources to build the Kingdom rather than wasting them on petty squabbles and criticisms.

As the Bible says in 1 Corinthians 3:16-17 (NIV), *"Don't you know that you are God's temple and that God's Spirit dwells in your midst? If anyone destroys God's temple, God will destroy that person, for God's temple is sacred, and you together are that temple."*

We are God's temple, and His Spirit dwells in us. We are called to be sacred and set apart for God's use. When we understand the value of Christ's sacrifice, we will want to live our lives in a way that reflects that sacredness.

The Bible says in Romans 14:8 (NIV), *"If we live, we live for the Lord; and if we die, we die for the Lord. So, whether we live or die, we belong to the Lord."*

We belong to the Lord and are called to live our lives in a way that reflects that belonging. Let's choose to live our lives for Him rather than for ourselves. Let's understand the true value of Christ's sacrifice and live our lives in a way that reflects that understanding.

Jesus Christ's sacrifice on the cross is of immense value. It is the foundation of our salvation and the source of our strength and inspiration. When we truly grasp the depth of Christ's love and the extent of His sacrifice, we will be motivated to live our lives in a way that honors Him.

Galatians 2:20 (NIV) says, *"I have been crucified with Christ, and I no longer live, but Christ lives in me. The life I now live in the body, I live by faith in the Son of God, who loved and gave himself for me."*

Unlocking Our True Value in Christ

Isaiah 53 vividly depicts Jesus Christ's sacrifice on the cross, where He was wounded and bruised for our transgressions, despised and rejected by men, pierced for our transgressions, and bore our sorrows and carried our pains. Despite all that He endured, Jesus does not want us to settle for less in our lives.

In John 10, Jesus describes Himself as the Good Shepherd who lays down His life for the sheep. He says, "*I came that they may have life and have it abundantly*" (John 10:10). Jesus' ultimate sacrifice was not just to save us from our sins, but to empower us to live an abundant life, reaching our greatest potential.

Jesus wants us to see the value He has placed in us and serve God with the best of everything. He wants us to be wild in purpose and pursuit, determined to soar, and be the best. This is in stark contrast to Satan's plan, which is to focus on our pains, mistakes, and failures, and settle for a mediocre life at best.

As the Good Shepherd, Jesus has a plan to lead us to our greatest potential. He says, "*My sheep hear my voice, and I know them, and they follow me*" (John 10:27). Jesus wants us to hear His voice and follow Him, trusting in His guidance and provision.

In John 10:10, Jesus says, "*The thief comes only to steal and kill and destroy. I came that they may have life and have it abundantly.*" Jesus is contrasting His plan for our lives with Satan's plan. While Satan seeks to steal, kill, and destroy, Jesus came to give us life and life abundantly.

The late Archbishop Benson Idahosa was a man of great passion and conviction. He was a leader who was unafraid to take a stand and challenge the status quo. This willingness to be controversial made him a man of great impact and influence.

He once said, "I would rather be controversial than inconsequential." This statement powerfully reminds us that a life of purpose and significance is often marked by controversy and challenge.

To be inconsequential means to be insignificant, to be

irrelevant, and to be ineffective. It means to live a life that makes no impact, leaves no legacy, and achieves nothing of lasting value.

On the other hand, being controversial means challenging the status quo, questioning established norms and conventions, and being willing to take a stand for what one believes in. It means being passionate, driven, and committed to making a difference.

Archbishop Benson Idahosa was passionate, driven, and committed to making a difference. Idahosa's life was marked by his passion for evangelism and his desire to spread the message of Christianity. He traveled extensively, conducting evangelistic crusades and ministering to large crowds. His charismatic personality and powerful sermons attracted a wide following, and he played a crucial role in the growth of the Pentecostal movement in Nigeria.

As a leader, Idahosa was unafraid to take a stand and challenge the status quo. He pioneered the Pentecostal movement in Nigeria, and signs, wonders, and miracles marked his ministry. He was also a strong educational advocate and founded Benson Idahosa University (BIU) in Benin City, Edo State, Nigeria.

Idahosa's legacy continues to inspire and empower leaders around the world. His life was a testament to the power of courage, conviction, and faith. Bringing back the statement he once said, "I would rather be controversial than inconsequential." This quote encapsulates his leadership approach and refusal to back down in adversity.
He was a man of purpose and significance.

As Christians, we are called to be people of purpose and significance. We are called to make a difference in the world, to be salt and light, and to bring glory to God. This often requires us to be controversial, challenge the status quo, and stand for our beliefs.

Of course, being controversial is not always easy. It can

be challenging, uncomfortable, and costly. But it is also advantageous. When willing to take a stand and challenge the status quo, we open ourselves to making a real difference and becoming the best and highest.

As the Bible says in Matthew 5:13-16 (NIV), "*You are the salt of the earth. But if the salt loses its saltiness, how can it be made salty again? It is no longer good for anything, except to be thrown out and trampled underfoot. You are the light of the world. A town built on a hill cannot be hidden. Neither do people light a lamp and put it under a bowl. Instead, they put it on its stand, and it gives light to everyone in the house.*"

As Christians, we are called to be the salt of the earth and the light of the world. We are called to make a difference, to bring flavor and light to a world that is often dark and flavorless. This requires us to be willing to take a stand, challenge the status quo, and be controversial.

So, let us not be afraid to be controversial, to take a stand, and to challenge the status quo. Doing so will make a real difference in the world and bring glory to God.

As the Bible says in 2 Timothy 1:7 (NIV), "*For the Spirit God gave us does not make us timid, but gives us power, love, and self-discipline.*" Let us not be timid, but let us be bold and courageous. Let us be willing to take a stand and challenge the status quo, for it is in doing so that we will make a real difference in the world and bring glory to God.

There is no room for conservatism in the Kingdom of God. We are called to be radical, to be bold, and to be fearless. We are called to reach for the highest honor and to never settle for less. When you need to be a lion, be one. When you need to be a lamb to one, don't bring out the virtue of a lamb where it is necessary to display the
virtue of a lion. Rise and roar! Don't be mediocre! Never!

So, let us look at the extravagant reward that Jesus has prepared for us. Let us look at the highest honor that He has called us to. Let us not allow the enemy to put people in our lives who will scare us away from our greatness. Instead, let us surround ourselves with people who will encourage, motivate, and push us to reach for the highest honor.

As we journey through life, remember that we are not just ordinary people. We are children of God, called to be ambassadors of Christ. We are called to represent God's Kingdom on earth and to bring glory to His name.

Let us not settle for a life that is mediocre at best. Instead, let us reach for the highest honor, be wild in purpose and pursuit, and be determined to soar. Let us be the best, and let us never settle for less.

As the Bible says in Philippians 3:14 (NIV), "*I press on toward the goal to win the prize for which God has called me heavenward in Christ Jesus.*"

Let us press on toward the goal, reach for the highest honor, and never settle for less. For we are children of God, called to be ambassadors of Christ, and we are destined for greatness.

Jesus Christ's sacrifice on the cross was not just about saving us from our sins; it was about giving us the opportunity to reach for the highest honor. He wants us to see the value He has placed in us and serve God with the best of everything.

Let us not settle for a life that is mediocre at best. Instead, let us reach for the highest honor, be wild in purpose and pursuit, and be determined to soar. For we are children of God, called to be ambassadors of Christ, and we are destined for greatness.

Coming into God's Presence with Confidence and Faith

Hebrews 4:16 encourages us to come boldly into God's presence, with confidence and faith, knowing that we will receive mercy and find grace to help us in our time of need. This passage speaks volumes of the perfect sacrifice of Jesus Christ and the privilege we have as believers to approach God's throne with boldness.

The Bible tells us that the blood of Jesus speaks better things than the blood of Abel (Hebrews 12:24). While the blood of Abel cried out for vengeance and justice, the blood of Jesus speaks of mercy, forgiveness, and redemption. This means that when we come into God's presence, the blood of Jesus is there to cleanse us and speak better things into our lives.

The perfect sacrifice of Jesus Christ has opened up a new and living way for us to approach God's throne (Hebrews 10:19-20). We no longer have to approach God with fear and trembling, but with confidence and faith, knowing that we have been made righteous through the blood of Jesus.

When we come into God's presence, we can be assured that we will receive mercy and find grace to help us in our time of need. This mercy and grace are not based on our own merits or works but on the perfect sacrifice of Jesus Christ. As the Bible says, *"For by one offering He has perfected for all time those who are sanctified"* (Hebrews 10:14).

The confidence we have in approaching God's throne is not based on our own righteousness but on the righteousness of Jesus Christ. As the Bible says, *"For our sake He made Him to be sin who knew no sin, so that in Him we might become the righteousness of God"* (2 Corinthians 5:21).

When we come into God's presence, we can be assured that we will receive mercy and find grace to help us become the greatest and highest version of ourselves. This is because the blood of Jesus speaks better things into our lives, things that will change the trajectory of our lives and cause us to become the best and highest.

When we do not lose faith and go before the Lord God in His courtroom, we must remember that our worthiness does not come from our deeds or actions but from the sacrifice of Jesus Christ our Lord. Let us not hesitate and rush to the Lord's
presence for we shall certainly receive mercy and grace

that is needed at that moment.

Seated with Christ in the Best and Highest Place

The Bible teaches us that Jesus Christ's sacrifice on the cross was not just an act of love and obedience but also a demonstration of His power and authority. As Philippians 2:9-11 (NIV) explains, "*Therefore God exalted him to the highest place and gave him the name that is above every name, that at the name of Jesus every knee should bow, in heaven and on earth and under the earth, and every tongue acknowledge that Jesus Christ is Lord, to the glory of God the Father.*"

Hebrews 1:3-4 (NIV) further emphasizes Jesus' exalted position, stating, "*The Son is the radiance of God's glory and the exact representation of his being, sustaining all things by his powerful word. After he had provided purification for sins, he sat down at the right hand of the Majesty in heaven.*"

Ephesians 1:20-22 (NIV) also highlights Jesus' exalted position, saying, "*He raised him from the dead and seated him at his right hand in the heavenly realms, far above all rule and authority, power and dominion, and every name that is invoked, not only in the present age but also in the one to come.*"

As believers, we are not just spectators of Jesus' exaltation but also participants. Colossians 3:1-3 (NIV) states, "*Since, then, you have been raised with Christ, set your hearts on things above, where Christ is, seated at the right hand of God. Set your minds on things above, not on earthly things. For you died, and your life is now hidden with Christ in God.*"

This means that we, as believers, have been placed by God in the best and highest place, just like Jesus. We have been seated with Christ in the heavenly realms, far above all rule and authority, power and dominion. Glory, Hallelujah!

There is a significant difference between those who have believed in their heart and those who confessed with their mouth that God raised Jesus from the dead. (Romans 10:9-10, NLT) - "*If you openly declare that Jesus is Lord and believe in your heart that God raised him from the dead, you will be saved. For it is by believing in your heart that you are made right with God, and it is by openly declaring your faith that you are saved."* And those who have not done so. The difference is not just about our eternal destiny; it is also about our present reality.

As believers, we don't sit in the same place as those who do not know Christ. It doesn't matter what status or position people may have in this world; as believers, we sit differently. We sit with Christ in the heavenly realms and have access to His power and authority.

So, if you have not yet understood the importance of believing and confessing the Lordship of Jesus, I encourage you to make a move today. Pray a simple prayer like this:

"Dear God, I believe that Jesus Christ is Your Son and that He died on the cross for my sins. I believe You raised Him from the dead and that He is now seated at Your right hand in the heavenly realms. I confess with my mouth that Jesus Christ is Lord, and I invite Him to be the Lord of my life. Thank You for saving and seating me with Christ in the heavenly realms. Amen."

If you have prayed this prayer, then congratulations! You are now seated with Christ in the best and highest place. Remember to set your heart and mind on things above, where Christ is, and to live your life by your new position in Christ.

As we conclude this chapter, we are reminded that as believers, we are expected to enjoy all the blessings associated with Jesus Christ's sacrifice. This includes becoming the best and the highest, just as Jesus was exalted to the highest place.

However, we must avoid being corrupted to attain this level of excellence. Corruption begins in the heart, and if our hearts are corrupt, we will never graduate to a place where God can use us for extraordinary things.

God wants to use all of us for His kingdom business, but not everyone will be used similarly. Some people may be used to make a financial impact, while others may be used for leadership, evangelism, construction, or other areas of ministry.

The key is to be available and willing to be used by God and to insist on mastering life so that we can be effective vessels for His use. If we don't insist on mastering life, we will constantly be garbage disposals, and our lives will not be worthy of emulation.

Satan's strategy is to fight against God's plan for our lives by making us irritated or making others irritated with us. But we must choose to be the unique person who holds God's heart.

We must allow God to purify us and give us a different perspective to do this. We must be willing to let go of our old ways of thinking and behaving and embrace God's new life for us.

In the upcoming chapters, we will address the five sins we must overcome to become the best and highest according to God's plan and purpose. These sins are:

1. **The Sin of Being a Hireling Instead of a Shepherd**: This sin involves prioritizing personal gain over serving others and fulfilling God's purpose.

2. **The Sin of Being a Wolf in Sheep's Clothing or Being a Sheep in Wolf's Clothing**: This sin involves pretending to be something you're not or failing to take a stand for what is right.

3. **The Sin of Ignoring, Neglecting, or Avoiding the Call to Sacrificial Living to advance God's Kingdom**: This sin involves refusing to make sacrifices or take risks to fulfill God's purpose and advance His kingdom.

4. **The Sin of Ignoring, Disrespecting, and Avoiding Divine Processes in Pursuit of God's Purpose and Plans for Your Life**: This sin involves ignoring or disobeying God's guidance and processes for achieving His purpose and plans.

5. **The Sin of Failure to Train Yourself to Know, Understand, and Respond to the Voice of the Shepherd**: This sin involves failing to develop a close relationship with God and to listen to and obey His voice.

We will explore these sins in detail and discuss how we can

overcome them to fulfill our destiny and become the best and highest version of ourselves.

CHAPTER THREE

The Sin That Hinders

"I don't understand myself at all, for I really want to do what is right, but I don't do it. Instead, I do the very thing I hate. I know perfectly well that what I am doing is wrong, and my bad conscience shows that I agree with these laws and know they are good. So I am not really the one doing these wrong things; it is sin living in me that does them." **Romans 7:15-17 (NLT)**

Sin is a hindrance that prevents us from becoming the best and the highest in life. It causes us to do what we don't want and brings hindrances that prevent us from fulfilling our potential.

So, what is sin? Sin is the transgression of God's will, either by omitting to do what God's law requires or by doing what it forbids. Transgression can occur in our thoughts and deeds. When we sin, we hinder God's will, and God's will is that we rise above mediocrity and become the best version of ourselves.

As discussed in the introduction of this book, God expects His people to be extraordinary, the best, and the highest. However, sin will not allow us to become the best versions of ourselves and to soar above mediocrity.

When we allow sin to reign in our lives, we settle for less than what God has intended for us. We become mediocre, and our lives are marked by stagnation and frustration.

But it doesn't have to be this way. We can overcome sin and its hindrances and become the best version of ourselves. As Paul wrote in Romans 8:37 (NIV), *"No, in all these things, we are more than conquerors through him who loved us."*

We are more than conquerors; we can overcome sin and its hindrances, rise above mediocrity, and become the best version of ourselves.

As we journey through this chapter and the following few chapters, we will explore the five sins that hinder us from becoming the best and the highest. We will discuss the sin of being a hireling instead of a shepherd, the sin of being a wolf in sheep's clothing or being a sheep in wolf's clothing, the sin of ignoring, neglecting, or avoiding the call to a sacrificial living to advance God's kingdom, the sin of ignoring, disrespecting, and avoiding divine processes in pursuit of God's purpose and plans for our lives, and the sin of failure to train ourselves to know, understand, and respond to the voice of the Shepherd.

We will delve into these sins and discuss how we can overcome them to fulfill our destiny and become our best and highest version.

Remember that God calls us to a higher, better, and more glorious place. He expects our lives to express a possibility, all of heaven. So, let us not settle for less. Let us go for the purest, highest, and best. Let us overcome the sin that hinders us and become the best version of ourselves.

As the Bible says in 2 Peter 3:14 (NIV), *"So then, dear friends, since you are looking forward to this, make every effort to be found spotless, blameless and at peace with him."* Let us be spotless, blameless, and at peace with God. Let us overcome the sin that hinders us and become the best versions of ourselves.

As I mentioned, sin hinders us from becoming the best and the highest version of ourselves. To illustrate the devastating consequences of the sin that hinders, let us examine the lives of some biblical characters who struggled with this issue.

King Saul, Israel's first monarch, is one example of such a figure.

Saul's life serves as a warning on how sin can keep us from reaching our greatest potential. Saul's life was characterized by bad choices and immoral actions that finally brought him to ruin, notwithstanding his early victories as king.

As we consider King Saul's story, let's focus on how the sin that prevented him impacted his life. Let us learn from his mistakes and apply the lessons to our lives to avoid the pitfalls that impeded Saul from being the finest and highest version of himself.

King Saul's Story: A Warning About the Sin That Hinders

The story of King Saul is a powerful example of the sin that hinders and its devastating consequences. Saul, the first king of Israel, was a man God had chosen to lead His people. However, despite his initial successes, Saul's life was marked by poor choices and sinful decisions that ultimately led to his downfall.

One of the most significant sins that hindered Saul was his disobedience to God's commands. In 1 Samuel 15, God instructed Saul to destroy the Amalekites, including their livestock. However, instead of obeying God's command, Saul decided to spare the best of the livestock, intending to use them for sacrifices.

This act of disobedience was a critical mistake with far-reaching consequences. When the prophet Samuel confronted Saul about his actions, Saul attempted to justify himself, claiming that he had spared the livestock to sacrifice them to God. However, Samuel saw through Saul's excuses and rebuked him, saying, "*To obey is better than sacrifice, and to heed is better than the fat of rams*" (1 Samuel 15:22).

Saul's disobedience was a sin that hindered him from becoming the best and highest version of himself. Despite his initial successes as king, Saul's life was marked by a series of failures and setbacks, ultimately leading to his downfall.

We can learn valuable lessons about the sin hindering King

Saul's narrative. First, it emphasizes how crucial it is to follow God's instructions. When we defy God, we expose ourselves to many detrimental outcomes, which may prevent us from reaching our full potential.

Secondly, the story of King Saul shows us that the sin that hinders can often be subtle and insidious. Saul's decision to spare the Amalekite livestock may have seemed minor at the time, but it ultimately led to his downfall.

Finally, the story of King Saul reminds us that the sin that hinders can have far- reaching consequences. Saul's disobedience not only affected his own life but also negatively impacted the entire nation of Israel.

As we reflect on the story of King Saul, let us remember the importance of obedience to God's commands and the dangers of the sin that hinders. Let us strive to become the best and highest version of ourselves and avoid the subtle and insidious sins that hinder us from achieving our full potential.

The Samson Story: An Account of Unrealized Promise

The story of Samson is another powerful example of the sin that hinders and its devastating consequences. Samson, a judge of Israel, was a man of extraordinary strength and potential. God set him apart from birth, and his parents were instructed to raise him as a Nazirite, dedicated to God's service.

However, despite his unique calling and potential, Samson's life was marked by sinful choices and decisions that ultimately led to his downfall. One of the most significant sins that hindered Samson was his lack of self-control and indulgence in fleshly desires.

In Judges 14, Samson is described as being attracted to a Philistine woman named Delilah. Although God had forbidden the Israelites from intermarrying with the Philistines, Samson ignored God's command and pursued a relationship with

Delilah.

This decision proved disastrous for Samson. The Philistine leaders bribed Delilah to discover the source of Samson's strength, manipulating and deceiving him, ultimately leading to his capture and blindness.

The story of Samson teaches us several important lessons about the sin that hinders. Firstly, it highlights the importance of self-control and discipline. Samson's lack of self-control and indulgence in fleshly desires led to his downfall.

Secondly, the story of Samson shows us that the sin that hinders can often be subtle and insidious. Samson's decision to pursue a relationship with Delilah may have seemed harmless, but it ultimately led to his capture and blindness.

Finally, the story of Samson reminds us that sin that hinders can have far-reaching consequences. Samson's sinful choices not only affected his own life but also negatively impacted the entire nation of Israel.

As we reflect on the story of Samson, let us remember the importance of self-control and discipline and the dangers of the sin that hinders. Let us strive to become the best and highest version of ourselves and avoid the subtle and insidious sins that hinder us from achieving our full potential.

The Story of Solomon: A Warning Against Compromise and Complacency

The story of Solomon, the third king of Israel, is another powerful example of the sin that hinders and has devastating consequences. Solomon, known for his wisdom and wealth, was a man God had blessed with extraordinary gifts and abilities.

However, despite his wisdom and wealth, Solomon's life was marked by sinful choices and decisions that ultimately led to his downfall. One of the most significant sins that hindered Solomon was his compromise and complacency.

In 1 Kings 11, Solomon is described as being influenced by his foreign wives, who turned his heart away from God. Despite God's clear instructions to the Israelites not to intermarry with the surrounding nations, Solomon ignored God's command and married many foreign women.

This decision proved to be disastrous for Solomon. His foreign wives introduced him to their pagan gods and practices, and Solomon began to compromise his faith and values. He built high places for his wives' gods and even sacrificed to them, which was a clear violation of God's commands.

The story of Solomon teaches us several important lessons about the sin that hinders. Firstly, it highlights the dangers of compromise and complacency. Solomon's decision to ignore God's commands and compromise his faith and values ultimately led to his downfall.

Secondly, the story of Solomon shows us that the sin that hinders can often be subtle and insidious. Solomon's compromise and complacency may have seemed harmless initially, but they ultimately led to his spiritual downfall.

Finally, the story of Solomon reminds us that sin that hinders can have far-reaching consequences. Solomon's sinful choices not only affected his own life but also negatively impacted the entire nation of Israel.

As we reflect on the story of Solomon, let us remember the importance of standing firm in our faith and values, as well as the dangers of compromise and complacency. Let us strive to become the best and highest version of ourselves and avoid the subtle and insidious sins that hinder us from achieving our full potential.

The Story of Gehazi: A Warning about Greed and Dishonesty

The story of Gehazi, the servant of the prophet Elisha, is another powerful example of the sin that hinders and has devastating consequences. Gehazi is mentioned in 2 Kings 5, where he is described as present when Elisha healed Naaman, the Syrian commander, of his leprosy.

After Naaman's healing, he offered Elisha a gift of silver, gold, and clothing, but Elisha refused to accept it. However, Gehazi, who had been watching the exchange, saw an opportunity to enrich himself and decided to pursue Naaman and ask for the gifts that Elisha had refused.

In 2 Kings 5:20-27, Gehazi's actions are described in detail. He runs after Naaman and asks for the gifts, claiming that Elisha had sent him. Unaware of Gehazi's deception, Naaman gives him the gifts, and Gehazi returns to Elisha's house, hiding the gifts and lying to Elisha about where he had been.

However, Elisha, who has been given spiritual insight into Gehazi's actions, confronts him about his deception and greed. As a result of his sin, Gehazi is struck with leprosy, and he is forced to live outside the camp, separated from the rest of the community.

The story of Gehazi teaches us several important lessons about the sin that hinders. Firstly, it highlights the dangers of greed and dishonesty. Gehazi's desire for wealth and material possessions led him to deceive and lie, ultimately resulting in his downfall.

Secondly, the story of Gehazi shows us that the sin that hinders can often be motivated by a desire for personal gain or advancement. Gehazi's actions were driven by his desire to enrich himself rather than by a desire to serve God or others.

Finally, the story of Gehazi reminds us that the sin that hinders can have severe consequences. Gehazi's deception and greed resulted in his physical and spiritual separation from the rest of the community, and it also brought shame and reproach to Elisha and the rest of the prophets.

As we reflect on Gehazi's story, let us remember the importance of living a life of integrity and honesty and the dangers of greed and dishonesty. Let us strive to become the best and highest version of ourselves and avoid the subtle and insidious sins that hinder us from achieving our full potential.

The Story of Ananias and Sapphira: A Warning of Deception and Dishonesty

The story of Ananias and Sapphira, a couple who were part of the early Christian church in Jerusalem, is another powerful example of the sin that hinders and its devastating consequences. God blessed Ananias and Sapphira with material possessions, and they decided to sell some of their property and give the proceeds to the church.

However, despite their outward appearance of generosity and devotion, Ananias and Sapphira hid a dark secret. They had decided to deceive the church and the apostles by keeping some of the money from selling their property for themselves.

In Acts 5, Peter confronts Ananias about his deception, saying, "*Ananias, why has Satan filled your heart to lie to the Holy Spirit and to keep back for yourself part of the proceeds of the land?*" (Acts 5:3).

Ananias' response to Peter's confrontation is telling. Instead of confessing his sin and seeking forgiveness, Ananias denies wrongdoing and attempts to justify his actions.

Tragically, Ananias' deception and dishonesty ultimately lead to his downfall. Peter pronounces judgment on Ananias, saying, "*You have not lied to men but to God*" (Acts 5:4). Ananias falls dead, and his wife Sapphira suffers the same fate when Peter confronts her about her role in the deception.

The story of Ananias and Sapphira teaches us several important lessons about the sin that hinders. Firstly, it highlights the dangers of deception and dishonesty. Ananias and Sapphira's decision to deceive the church and the apostles ultimately led to their downfall.

Secondly, the story of Ananias and Sapphira shows us that the sin that hinders can often be hidden behind a mask of outward devotion and religiosity. Ananias and Sapphira appeared devout and generous church members, but they were hiding a dark secret of deception and dishonesty.

Finally, the story of Ananias and Sapphira reminds us that the sin that hinders can have severe consequences. Ananias and Sapphira's deception and dishonesty ultimately led to their physical death, and it also brought shame and reproach to the church.

As we reflect on the story of Ananias and Sapphira, let us remember the importance of honesty and integrity and the dangers of deception and dishonesty. Let us strive to become the best and highest version of ourselves and avoid the subtle and insidious sins that hinder us from achieving our full potential.

The Story of Demas: A Warning about Worldliness and Apostasy

The story of Demas, a companion of the apostle Paul, is another powerful example of the sin that hinders and has devastating consequences. Demas is mentioned in several of Paul's epistles, including Colossians 4:14, Philemon 1:24, and 2 Timothy 4:10.

Initially, Demas was a faithful companion of Paul and a devoted follower of Christ. However, over time, Demas began to be drawn away from his faith by the world's allurements. In 2 Timothy 4:10, Paul writes, "*Demas, because he loved this world, has deserted me and has gone to Thessalonica.*"

Demas' love for the world led him to abandon his faith and relationship with Paul. This is a classic example of the sin that hinders where a person's desire for worldly pleasures and pursuits leads them to compromise their faith and values.

The story of Demas teaches us several important lessons about sin and its hindrance. First, it highlights the dangers of worldliness and the allurements of sin. Demas's love for the world led him to abandon his faith and relationship with Paul.

Secondly, the story of Demas shows us that the sin that hinders can often be a gradual process. Demas did not suddenly abandon his faith; instead, the world's allurements gradually drew him away from it.

Finally, the story of Demas reminds us that the sin that hinders can have severe consequences. Demas' abandonment of his faith led to his spiritual death, and it also brought shame and reproach to the church.

As we reflect on the story of Demas, let us remember the importance of guarding our hearts against the allurements of the world and the dangers of sin. Let us strive to become the best and highest version of ourselves and avoid the subtle and insidious sins that hinder us from achieving our full potential.

As we conclude this chapter, we are reminded that sin hinders every believer who desires greatness. Through the stories of King Saul, Ananias and Sapphira, Demas, Samson, and others, we have seen the devastating consequences of sin and how it can prevent us from achieving our full potential.

We have learned that sin that hinders can take many forms, including disobedience, deception, dishonesty, worldliness, and complacency. It can often be subtle and insidious, masquerading as harmless or good.

However, we have also learned that overcoming the sins that hinder us is possible. By studying the requirements of our positions in life, whether in marriage, ministry, or any other area, we can avoid the pitfalls that hinder us from achieving greatness.

As the Bible says in 2 Timothy 2:15, "*Be diligent to present yourself approved to God, a worker who does not need to be ashamed, rightly dividing the word of truth.*" We must
diligently study and apply God's word to our lives to avoid the sin

that hinders us and achieve greatness.

The stories shared in this chapter have taught us valuable lessons about the importance of living a life of obedience, integrity, and honesty. They have shown us that sin can have devastating consequences but also reminded us that overcoming sin and achieving greatness is possible.

As we progress toward greatness, let us remember the importance of studying our position requirements. Whether seeking to excel in our careers, marriages, or ministries, we must diligently study and apply God's word.

As the Bible says in Hosea 4:6, "*My people are destroyed for lack of knowledge.*" We must not allow a lack of knowledge to hinder us from achieving greatness. Instead, we must study and apply God's word to our lives to avoid the sin that hinders us and achieve greatness.

The remaining chapters will examine the six sins I identified hindering believers who desire greatness. By understanding and overcoming these sins, we can avoid the hindrances that prevent us from achieving greatness and fulfilling our destiny as children of God. Let us move forward in our journey toward greatness with the knowledge and understanding of the sins that hinder us.

CHAPTER FOUR

The Sin of Being a Hireling Instead of a Shepherd

In John 10:11-12, Jesus says, "*I am the good shepherd. The good shepherd lays down his life for the sheep. The hired hand is not the shepherd and does not own the sheep. So when he sees the wolf coming, he abandons the sheep and runs away*" (NIV). In this passage, Jesus clearly explains the difference between a hireling and a shepherd.

A hireling is a paid worker or employee. In Bible times, a hireling could be hired for as little as one day, or they might contract to work for more extended periods. A hireling's primary motivation is personal gain, and they often prioritize their interests over the well-being of those they are supposed to care for.

On the other hand, a shepherd is a person who takes care of sheep. Sheep are curious but dumb animals, often unable to find their way home even if the sheepfold is within sight. Knowing this fault, the shepherd never takes his eyes off their wandering sheep. "*I will instruct you and teach you in the way you should go; I will counsel you with My eye upon you.*" (Psalm 32:8 AMP) Often, sheep wander into a briar patch or fall over a cliff in the rugged Palestinian hills. The shepherd tenderly searches for their sheep and carries them to safety. "*And when he gets home, he calls together his friends and his neighbors, saying to them, 'Rejoice with me, because I have found my sheep that was lost!'*" (Luke 15:6 AMP)

In water-hungry Syria and Palestine, shepherds have always had to search diligently for water, sometimes for hours daily. Sheep must be watered daily. The shepherd might find a bubbling stream for the sheep, who are always on the move and need fresh pastures daily. *"He makes me to lie down in green pastures; He leads me beside*
the still waters." (Psalm 23:2 NKJV) A trusted shepherd provides loving protection for the flock. The presence of the shepherd also offers comfort to the flock.

The key difference between a hireling and a shepherd is their motivation and level of commitment. A hireling is motivated by personal gain and has a limited commitment to the flock. On the other hand, a shepherd is motivated by a desire to care for and protect the flock and has a deep commitment to the well-being of the sheep.

Jesus said, *"The hired hand is not the shepherd and does not own the sheep. So when he sees the wolf coming, he abandons the sheep and runs away"* (John 10:12 NIV). A hireling's lack of commitment and motivation means they will often abandon their responsibilities when things get tough.

In contrast, a shepherd will lay down their life for the sheep. Jesus said, *"I am the good shepherd. The good shepherd lays down his life for the sheep"* (John 10:11 NIV). A
shepherd's commitment to the flock is unwavering, and they are willing to make sacrifices for the well-being of the sheep.

In the context of our Christian walk, being a hireling instead of a shepherd can manifest in many ways. It can mean prioritizing personal gain over serving others and fulfilling God's purpose. It can mean being motivated by selfish desires rather than a desire to care for and protect others. It can mean having a limited commitment to God's work and abandoning our responsibilities when things get tough.

As we reflect on our lives and motivations, let us ask ourselves: Are we hirelings or shepherds? Are we motivated by personal gain or a desire to serve and care for others? Are we willing to lay down our lives for the sake of others, or are we more concerned with our interests?

Let us strive to be shepherds, motivated by a desire to care for and protect others and willing to make sacrifices for the well-being of those around us. Let us avoid the sin of being hirelings and instead seek to serve others and fulfill God's purpose with humility, compassion, and commitment.

As we continue on our journey toward greatness, we must be aware of the sins that can hinder us from achieving our full potential. This chapter will help us discuss intensely the sin of being a hireling instead of a shepherd.

One example of someone in the Bible who prioritized personal gain over serving others and fulfilling God's purpose is Balaam. Balaam was a prophet hired by King Balak of Moab to curse the Israelites. Despite being warned by God not to curse the Israelites, Balaam was motivated by the promise of personal gain and decided to go ahead with the curse.

However, as Balaam was on his way to meet King Balak, his donkey saw an angel of the Lord standing on the road and refused to move. Balaam beat the donkey three times before the Lord opened the donkey's mouth, and it spoke to Balaam, saying, "*What have I done to you to make you beat me these three times?*" (Numbers 22:28).

Balaam's response to the donkey's question reveals his true motivation. He says, "*You have made me look like a fool! If only I had a sword in my hand, I would kill you right now!*" (Numbers 22:29). Balaam's response shows that he was more concerned with his personal gain than with serving God or fulfilling His purpose.

The story of Balaam teaches us the importance of prioritizing God's purpose over personal gain. When we prioritize personal gain, we can become like Balaam, who was willing to curse the Israelites for a price. However, when we prioritize God's purpose, we can become like the shepherd who lays down his life for the sheep (John 10:11).

The heart of the matter is the matter of the heart. What motivates us? Is it personal gain or a desire to serve others? The Bible says in Matthew 6:21, "*For where your treasure is, there your heart will be also*" (NIV). Our hearts are drawn to what we treasure most. If we treasure personal gain, our hearts will be drawn to it. But if we treasure serving others and fulfilling God's purpose, our hearts will be drawn to it.

There are people whose greatness failed because they, unfortunately, committed a significant greatness error: the sin of a hireling. Judas Iscariot is another excellent example of someone in the Bible who prioritized personal gain over serving others and fulfilling God's purpose.

Judas was one of Jesus' twelve apostles but was motivated by personal gain. As the Bible says in John 12:6, "*He did not say this because he cared about the poor but because he was a thief; as keeper of the money bag, he used to help himself to what was put into it*" (NIV). Judas' love of money and personal gain ultimately led him to betray Jesus for thirty pieces of silver.

The story of Judas teaches us the importance of prioritizing God's purpose over personal gain. When we prioritize personal gain, we can become like Judas, who was willing to betray Jesus for a price. However, when we prioritize God's purpose, we can become like the shepherd who lays down his life for the sheep (John 10:11).

As the Bible says in 1 Corinthians 13:3, "*If I give all I possess to the poor and surrender my body to the flames, but have not love, I gain nothing.*" If our motivation is personal gain, our actions are worthless, no matter how noble they seem.

The Characteristics of a Shepherd: A Study of John 10

In John 10, Jesus describes Himself as the Good Shepherd, highlighting the characteristics that distinguish Him from a hireling.

The Shepherd Enters Through the Door

Jesus says, "*I tell you the truth. The man who does not enter the sheep pen through the gate but climbs in by some other way, is a thief and a robber*" (John 10:1 ERV). A true shepherd enters the sheep pen through the gate, not by climbing in through another way.

This illustrates the shepherd's commitment to following the proper path, even if it's more difficult. A hireling, on the other hand, might look for an easier way in, even if it means breaking the rules.

The Shepherd Knows His Sheep

Jesus continues, "*The man who enters through the gate is the shepherd of the sheep. The gatekeeper opens the gate for him, and the sheep listen to his voice. He calls his own sheep by name and leads them out*" (John 10:2-3 ERV). A true shepherd knows his sheep intimately, calling them by name and leading them out.

This highlights the shepherd's relationship with his sheep. A hireling, on the other hand, might not take the time to get to know the sheep individually.

The Shepherd Leads the Sheep Out

Jesus says, "*When he has brought out all his own sheep, he walks ahead of them. They follow him because they know his voice*" (John 10:4 ERV). A true shepherd leads the sheep out, walking ahead of them and guiding them.

This illustrates the shepherd's leadership and guidance. A hireling, on the other hand, might not be willing to take the lead or guide the sheep.

The Shepherd Lays Down His Life

Jesus concludes, "*I am the good shepherd. The good shepherd gives his life for the sheep. But the hired man, who is not a shepherd and does not own the sheep, sees the wolf coming and leaves the sheep and runs away. Then the wolf attacks the sheep and scatters them"* (John 10:11-12 ERV). A true shepherd lays down his life for the sheep, while a hireling runs away in the face of danger.

This highlights the shepherd's willingness to sacrifice himself for the sake of his sheep. A hireling, on the other hand, is more concerned with his safety and well- being.

Comparing The Characteristics of a Hireling and a Shepherd

As we discussed earlier, the sin of being a hireling instead of a shepherd is a major greatness error that can hinder us from achieving our full potential. A hireling is motivated by personal gain, whether financial reward, power, position, or notoriety. They work solely for the pay and have no personal investment in the well-being of those they are supposed to care for.

As the Bible says in John 10:12-13, "*A hired hand is not a shepherd and doesn't care about the sheep. When he sees a wolf coming, he runs for it, leaving the sheep to be attacked and scattered. He runs because he is a hired hand and doesn't care about the sheep"* (TLB). The characteristics of a hireling show they are motivated by personal gain and have no personal investment in the well-being of those they are supposed to care for.

On the other hand, a shepherd is motivated by a desire to care for and protect others. They are willing to lay down their lives for the sake of those they are responsible for, and they have a deep personal investment in their well-being.

Jesus in John 10:11 says, "*I am the good shepherd. The good shepherd lays down his life for the sheep"* (NIV). Jesus used these words to highlight the characteristics of a shepherd: to be motivated by a desire to care for and protect others and is willing to lay down their life for the sake of those they are responsible for.

One of the major flaws of a hireling is their tendency to be irresponsible when it is time to take responsibility. They flee or run away when faced with challenges or difficulties rather than standing firm and fighting for what is right. They allow the "wolves" or obstacles to interfere with their responsibility rather than finding ways to overcome them.

For example, in 1 Samuel 17, we see the story of David and Goliath. The Israelite army faced the challenge of fighting against the Philistines, but they were afraid and ran away. However, David, a shepherd, stood firm and fought against Goliath, trusting in God's power and protection.

Another characteristic of a hireling is their lack of attention to detail. They ignore that the "wolf" chasing the flock wants to eat the flock, and they neglect their responsibility to care for the little things in the kingdom of God. They may start a project or initiative but quickly lose interest and abandon it, leaving others to pick up the pieces.

For example, in Matthew 25:14-30, we see the parable of the talents. A master gave his servants different amounts of talents, and they were expected to use them wisely. However, one of the servants, who was like a hireling, buried his talent in the ground and did not use it to benefit the master. When the master returns, he is angry with the servant and takes away his talent.

Hirelings also tend to view anyone who tries to hold them accountable or correct them as enemies. They become defensive and resistant to feedback rather than being open to constructive criticism and willing to learn from their mistakes.

For example, in 1 Kings 13, we see the story of a prophet sent by God to speak against the altar at Bethel. However, when the prophet spoke against the altar, King Jeroboam became angry and tried to arrest him. The prophet, who was like a hireling, became defensive and resistant to feedback, and he did not listen to the king's warning.

In contrast, a shepherd is willing to take responsibility and stand firm in the face of challenges. They are attentive to detail and take their responsibility to care for the flock seriously. They are willing to listen to feedback and correction, and they are humble and willing to learn from their mistakes.

As believers, we must purge ourselves from the sin of being hirelings. We must recognize that our motivation and actions have consequences and are responsible for caring for and protecting those around us. We must be willing to take responsibility, stand firm in the face of challenges, and be attentive to detail.

We must also recognize that Satan is always trying to hire us, to motivate us by personal gain rather than a desire to serve and care for others. We must resist his attempts and instead seek to be motivated by a desire to serve and care for others.

As the Bible says in 1 Peter 5:8, "*Be alert and of sober mind. Your enemy, the devil, prowls around like a roaring lion looking for someone to devour*" (NIV). We must be alert and aware of Satan's attempts to hire us, resist his attempts, and instead seek to be motivated by a desire to serve and care for others.

Let us pray as believers and purge ourselves of the hireling mentality. Let us deal with the wolves, both within and outside the body of Christ. Let us seek to be shepherds motivated by a desire to care for and protect others and willing to lay down their lives for the sake of those they are responsible for.

As the Bible says in John 10:14-15, "*I am the good shepherd; I know my sheep, and my sheep know me—just as the Father knows me and I know the Father—and I lay down my life for the sheep*" (NIV). Let us seek to be like Jesus, the good shepherd who laid down his life for the sake of humanity.

We must also recognize that being a shepherd is not just a title or a position but a lifestyle. It requires us to be willing to serve and care for others, even when challenging. It requires us to be willing to lay down our lives for the sake of those we are responsible for.

As the Bible says in Philippians 2:3-4, "*Do nothing out of selfish ambition or vain conceit. Rather, in humility value others above yourselves, not looking to your own interests but each of you to the interests of the others*" (NIV). Let us seek to be humble, value others above ourselves, and look to the interests of others rather than our interests.

Let us purge ourselves from the sin of being hirelings and seek to be shepherds motivated to care for and protect others. Let us be willing to lay down our lives for the sake of those we are responsible for, seek humility, and value others above ourselves.

As the Bible says in Matthew 20:26-28, "*Whoever wants to become great among you must be your servant, and whoever wants to be first must be your slave—just as the Son of Man did not come to be served, but to serve, and to give his life as a ransom for many*" (NIV). Let us seek to be servants and enslaved people, and let us strive to give our lives as a ransom for many.

The Attitude of a Hireling in the Church

In the church, a hireling is motivated by personal gain, whether financial reward, power, position, or notoriety. They are more concerned with their interests and ambitions than with serving and caring for God's flock.

The attitude of a hireling in the church is characterized by a lack of commitment and dedication to the congregation's well-being. They are more concerned with their status and reputation than with the spiritual growth and development of the people they should serve.

For example, in Acts 20:29-30, Paul warns the church elders in Ephesus about the dangers of hirelings in the church. He says, "*I know that after I leave, savage wolves will come in among you and will not spare the flock. Even from your own number, men will arise and distort the truth in order to draw away disciples after them*" (NIV).

In this passage, Paul warns the elders about the dangers of hirelings who will arise from within the church and seek to draw away disciples after themselves. These hirelings are motivated by a desire for power and control rather than to serve and care for God's flock.

Another example of a hireling in the church is Diotrephes,

mentioned in 3 John 9-10. Diotrephes was a leader in the church who loved to be in charge and to have the preeminence. He refused to welcome the apostle John and other believers and even went so far as to cast them out of the church.

In this passage, John describes Diotrephes as a hireling motivated by a desire for power and control. He says, "*I wrote to the church, but Diotrephes, who loves to be in charge, does not acknowledge our authority*" (NIV).

The consequences of being a hireling in the church are severe. When we are motivated by personal gain and a desire for power and control, we can cause harm and division within the body of Christ.

For example, in 1 Corinthians 1:10-13, Paul addresses the divisions and quarrels that were taking place within the church in Corinth. He says, "*I appeal to you, brothers and sisters, in the name of our Lord Jesus Christ, that all of you agree with one another in what you say and that there be no divisions among you, but that you be perfectly united in mind and thought*" (NIV). Paul is addressing the consequences of being a hireling in the church. When we are motivated by personal gain and a desire for power and control, we can cause divisions and quarrels within the body of Christ.

A hireling's attitude in the church is characterized by a lack of commitment to the congregation's well-being. They are more concerned with their interests and ambitions than serving and caring for God's flock.

The Consequences of Being a Hireling

As we discussed earlier, being a hireling instead of a shepherd is a significant greatness error that can hinder us from achieving greatness. This section will examine the consequences of being a hireling and how it can hinder us from achieving greatness in the kingdom of God, the business world, and our various families.

One of the consequences of being a hireling is a lack

of commitment and dedication. When we are motivated by personal gain, we are more likely to abandon our responsibilities when things get tough. This can lead to a lack of trust and confidence in our abilities and ultimately hinder us from achieving greatness.

For example, in the business world, a hireling may be more concerned with meeting sales targets and earning a commission than providing excellent customer service and building long-term relationships with clients. This can lead to a lack of customer loyalty and retention, ultimately hindering the business from achieving greatness.

In the kingdom of God, a hireling may be more concerned with gaining recognition and prestige than serving and caring for others. This can lead to a lack of fruitfulness and effectiveness in ministry, ultimately hindering the kingdom's advancement.

Another consequence of being a hireling is a lack of accountability and responsibility. When motivated by personal gain, we are more likely to shift the blame and avoid taking responsibility for our actions. This can lead to a lack of trust and confidence in our abilities and ultimately hinder us from achieving greatness.

For example, in our families, a hireling may be more concerned with avoiding conflict and maintaining peace rather than taking responsibility for their actions and being accountable to their family members. This can lead to a lack of respect and trust within the family, ultimately hindering the family from achieving greatness.

In the business world, a hireling may be more concerned with covering up their mistakes and avoiding accountability than taking responsibility for their actions and being transparent with their clients and colleagues. This can lead to a lack of trust and confidence in the business and ultimately hinder the business from achieving greatness.

A third consequence of being a hireling is a lack of vision and purpose. When motivated by personal gain, we are more likely to focus on short-term gains and immediate gratification rather than long-term vision and purpose. This can lead to a lack of direction and focus, ultimately hindering us from achieving greatness.

For example, in the kingdom of God, a hireling may be more concerned with building their ministry and empire rather than advancing the kingdom and fulfilling God's purpose. This can lead to a lack of unity and cooperation among believers, ultimately hindering the kingdom's advancement.

In the business world, a hireling may be more concerned with making a quick profit and advancing their career than building a sustainable and successful business that benefits others. This can lead to a lack of innovation and progress, ultimately hindering the business from achieving greatness.

Being a hireling instead of a shepherd can have serious consequences that hinder us from achieving greatness in the kingdom of God, the business world, and our various families. Let us seek to be shepherds motivated by a desire to serve and care for others and willing to take responsibility and be accountable for our actions. Let us seek a long-term vision and purpose and strive to build sustainable and successful relationships and organizations that benefit others.

Overcoming the Sin of Being a Hireling Instead of a Shepherd

In John 10, Jesus distinguishes between a shepherd and a hireling, pointing out the characteristics of a true shepherd. On the other hand, a hireling is motivated by self- interest and lacks a genuine concern for the sheep. As believers, we must be careful not to fall into the sin of being a hireling instead of a shepherd.

To overcome this sin, we must first recognize the characteristics of a hireling and then take practical steps to align ourselves with the characteristics of a true shepherd.

Recognizing the Characteristics of a Hireling

A hireling is motivated by self-interest and lacks a genuine concern for the sheep. They are more concerned with their welfare and safety than with the well-being of the sheep. Jesus says, "*The hired hand is not the shepherd and does not own the sheep. So when he sees the wolf coming, he abandons the sheep and runs away*" (John 10:12-13). A hireling will abandon the sheep in times of danger, seeking to save their skin.

Practical Steps to Overcome the Sin of Being a Hireling

So, how can we overcome the sin of being a hireling instead of a shepherd? Let me share some practical steps, based on Scripture:

Learn to recognize the Shepherd's voice: Jesus says, "*My sheep listen to my voice; I know them, and they follow me*" (John 10:27). We must learn to recognize the Shepherd's voice, which is characterized by love, care, and sacrifice.

Spend time with the Shepherd: The more time we spend with the Shepherd, the more we learn to recognize His voice. Spend time reading God's Word, praying, and seeking His guidance.

Examine your motivations: Ask yourself why you are serving or leading. Is it for personal gain or recognition, or is it out of a genuine love for God and His people? This will help you to know if the virtues of a hireling are manifesting in you, then you can put it off.

Seek accountability: Surround yourself with people who will hold you accountable and encourage you to follow the Shepherd's voice.

Practice humility and selflessness: A true shepherd is characterized by humility and selflessness. Practice putting others before yourself and seeking to serve rather than be served.

Be willing to lay down your life: Jesus says, "*I am the* *good shepherd. The good shepherd lays down his life for the sheep"* (John 10:11). Be willing to lay down your life for the sake of others, just as Jesus did.

Trust in the Shepherd's provision: Jesus says, *"I came that they may have life and have it abundantly"* (John 10:10). Trust in the Shepherd's provision and care for you, rather than seeking to provide for yourself.

Follow the Shepherd's example: Jesus says, *"I am the good shepherd. I know my own and my own know me"* (John 10:14). Follow the Shepherd's example, seeking to know and care for those under your care.

I am convinced that if we follow these practical steps, we can overcome the sin of being a hireling instead of a shepherd. Let us seek to recognize the Shepherd's voice, spend time with Him, and practice humility and selflessness as we serve God and His people.

The Importance of Accountability

Accountability is a crucial aspect of overcoming the sin of being a hireling. Surrounding yourself with people who will hold you accountable and encourage you to follow the Shepherd's voice can help you stay on track.

As Proverbs 27:17 says, *"Iron sharpens iron, and one man sharpens another."* Accountability can help sharpen us, making us more effective servants of God.

The Role of Humility and Selflessness

Humility and selflessness are essential characteristics of a true shepherd. Practicing these qualities can help us overcome the sin of being a hireling.

As Philippians 2:3-4 says, *"Do nothing from selfish ambition or conceit, but in humility count others more significant than yourselves. Let each of you look not only to your interests but also to the interests of others."*

By practicing humility and selflessness, we can become more like the Good Shepherd, who laid down His life for the sheep.

Overcoming the sin of being a hireling instead of a shepherd requires a deep commitment to following the Shepherd's voice. By recognizing the characteristics of a hireling

My Counsel: Listening to the Voice of the Shepherd

As believers, we are constantly bombarded with various voices that seek to influence our thoughts, emotions, and actions. One of the most subtle and deceptive voices is that of the hireling, who comforts us in mediocrity. However, I urge every believer to tune in to the voice of the Shepherd, who prepares us for greatness beyond our call- up duty.

The Voice of the Hireling

The voice of the hireling is one that comforts us in mediocrity. It is a voice that tells us that we are doing enough, that we are good enough, and that we don't need to strive for more.

The voice of the hireling is a seductive one, as it appeals to our fleshly desires for comfort, security, and ease. However, this voice is not from God, and it will ultimately lead us down a path of stagnation and complacency.

The Voice of the Shepherd

The voice of the Shepherd is one that prepares us for greatness beyond our call-up duty. It is a voice that challenges us, encourages us, and empowers us to become all that God has called us to be.

The voice of the Shepherd is a voice of comfort and upliftment, but it is not a voice that comforts us in mediocrity. Rather, it is a voice that comforts us in our struggles, our challenges, and our weaknesses. It is a voice that reminds us that we are not alone, that we are not abandoned, and that we are not forsaken.

The voice of the Shepherd prepares us for greatness beyond our call-up duty. It prepares us for the wolf, for the lion, for the bear, and for every other challenge that we may face in life.

The voice of the Shepherd reminds us that we are not just

ordinary people, but we are people of destiny, people of purpose, and people of power. It reminds us that we have been called to greatness and that we have been equipped with everything we need to achieve that greatness.

I urge every believer to tune in to the voice of the Shepherd, who prepares us for greatness beyond our call-up duty. Let us reject the voice of the hireling, which comforts us in mediocrity, and instead, let us listen to the voice of the Shepherd, which challenges us, encourages us, and empowers us to become all that God has called us to be.

> *"When he has brought out all his own sheep, he walks ahead of them and they will follow him, for they are familiar with his voice. But they will run away from strangers and never follow them, for they don't recognize the voice of strangers. Jesus told them this parable, but they didn't understand what he meant. So Jesus explained it to them: 'I tell you the truth, I am the gate for the sheep'."* John 10:4-8 (TPT)

Purging the Sin of Being a Hireling

As we conclude this chapter on "The Sin of Being a Hireling Instead of a Shepherd," we are faced with a critical choice: will we continue to operate with a hireling mentality, or will we purge ourselves of this sin and become the gold that God desires us to be?

The journey ahead of us is crucial, and it requires us to fight against Satan's ability to hire us. We must remember that Satan hired Judas Iscariot, and today he is nowhere to be found. We do not want to suffer the same fate.

Instead, we want to become like the stone that the builders rejected, which becomes the chief cornerstone. We want to maintain our place and outgrow it, becoming a force to be reckoned with in the kingdom of God.

So, we must pray as believers and purge ourselves of the hireling mentality. We must deal with the wolves that seek to attack our congregation and the body of Christ.

As we purge ourselves of the sin of being a hireling, we will become more like Jesus, the Good Shepherd. We will learn to recognize His voice and follow Him, even in the face of danger or adversity.

Let us commit to purging ourselves of the hireling mentality and become the gold that God desires us to be. Let us pray:

"Dear Heavenly Father, I come before You today, acknowledging the sin of being a hireling in my life. I recognize that I have been motivated by self-interest and a desire for personal gain, rather than a genuine concern for Your people.

"I ask that You would purge me of this sin and help me to become more like Jesus, the Good Shepherd. Give me a heart that is willing to lay down my life for the sake of Your people.

"Help me to recognize Your voice and follow You, even in the face of danger or adversity. Give me the courage to stand against the wolves that seek to attack Your people.

"I pray that You would raise me and make me a force to be reckoned with in Your kingdom. Use me to bring glory to Your name and to advance Your kingdom on earth.

"In Jesus' name, I pray. Amen."

CHAPTER FIVE

The Sin of Being a Wolf in Sheep's Clothing or a Sheep in Wolf's Clothing

A story was once told about a Thursday morning reading session between a father and his 8-year-old son, Ethan. On this particular Thursday, Ethan brought in a book about Little Red Riding Hood, but with a twist - it was written from the wolf's perspective.

As Ethan read the story, he began to realize that the wolf was trying to manipulate him into believing that he was trying to help Grandma. But Ethan was not convinced. He looked up at his dad and said, "I think he's lying." His dad couldn't help but laugh out loud and replied, "I think so too, Ethan."

As they continued reading the story, their suspicions were confirmed. Despite the wolf's attempts to disguise himself as Grandma, his true nature was eventually revealed. He tried to eat Little Red Riding Hood, and when confronted, he simply said, "I'm a wolf. I couldn't help myself."

This story highlights the nature of wolves, who are natural predators driven to devour their prey. If a wolf were to show up at your door, it would be bad news. No one would mistake a snarling wolf for a cute little puppy.

During the reading session, Ethan had astutely observed that the wolf tried to disguise himself. This serves as a valuable lesson for all of us, reminding us to be cautious of those who may try to disguise their true intentions.

Scripture has a lot to say about wolves, and it's never good.

Wolves are treacherous and dangerous when presented in God's Word. Jesus warns us about the dangers of wolves in sheep's clothing, saying: *"Watch out for false prophets. They come to you in sheep's clothing, but inwardly they are ferocious wolves."* (Matthew 7:15)

This warning from Jesus is spiritual straight talk, and it comes right after He describes two ways of life: one that leads to eternal life and one that leads to destruction. On the road of life, it's easy to get lulled into complacency, to lose sight of the finish line. It's easy to be turned aside, to backslide in our faith, unless we "watch out." Have you ever known someone who was on fire for Christ, dedicated to following Him and His Word, but now they're not?

What happened? They stopped watching out. They suddenly started sinning being a sheep in wolf's clothing in this case. Instead of being self-controlled and alert, their enemy, Satan, prowled into their life like a roaring lion, seeking to devour them. And
he probably used other people to turn them aside - people who taught false truths, false prophets.

We don't stay on the narrow road by accident; we stay on it by being guided by Jesus and His Word. It's why Jesus says, "Watch out...heads up...be alert for those who would lead you off my path of life, watch out...heads up... be alert for those who will lead you out of the way of becoming the best and the highest." (Paraphrase mine)

But Jesus tells us what to watch out for - or maybe better put, "who" to watch out for.

The Deception of Wolves in Sheep's Clothing

Let's ask an important question: What is the most important and probably the most dangerous priority of a shepherd?

We'd all agree it's protecting the flock, guarding his sheep. If a wolf shows up snarling and frothing at the mouth, stepping between him and his sheep is his duty, but it's also dangerous.

But Jesus describes an even more dangerous situation—what if a wolf quietly slips in among the sheep, covered in fleece and disguised as one of them?

This is what false prophets and false teachers do. The Apostle Paul also knew this would be one of the greatest dangers for God's shepherds, saying:

"I know that after I leave, savage wolves will come among you and not spare the flock. Even from your own number, men will arise and distort the truth in order to draw away disciples after them. So be on your guard!" (Acts 20:29-31a)

Be on your guard...watch out! Heads up!

In the introductory part of this Chapter, we will be having a look at the concept of being a sheep in wolf's clothing and a wolf in sheep's clothing before we proceed to look at the sin of being a wolf in sheep's clothing or a sheep in wolf's clothing. This concept is closely related to Jesus' warning in Matthew 7:15, where He cautions His followers to "*beware of false prophets, who come to you in sheep's clothing but inwardly are ravenous wolves.*"

Jesus' statement points to the danger of deception and the importance of discernment. As we journey towards becoming the greatest and highest version of ourselves, we must understand the tactics of false prophets and learn to discern their fruit. We do not only need to understand the tactics of false prophets and learn to discern their fruit, we must also not be involved in the sin of having a false identity.

The Sin of Being a Wolf in Sheep's Clothing

In Matthew 7:15, Jesus employs a familiar idiom to convey a vital message: "*Beware of false prophets, who come to you in sheep's clothing but inwardly are ravenous wolves.*" This warning is nestled within a broader context, where Jesus instructs His listeners to "*Enter through the narrow gate*" (Matthew 7:13), emphasizing the importance of embracing a counter-cultural path that leads to life.

In contrast, Jesus notes that the wide gate and broad road, which many traverse, ultimately lead to destruction. This was particularly relevant to the religious elite of Jesus' time, some of whom were themselves wolves in sheep's clothing. Jesus' words serve as a stark reminder that the life path is narrow and less traveled, while the road to destruction is broad and appealing to many.

Later, in John 10, Jesus expands on this idea, stating, *"Very truly I tell you Pharisees, anyone who does not enter the sheep pen by the gate but climbs in by some other way, is a thief and a robber"* (John 10:1). This imagery would have resonated with Jesus' audience, who were familiar with the local shepherds and the popular Aesop's fable that cautioned them to remain vigilant.

So, how can we discern who to trust? Jesus provides a clear answer: whereas false shepherds are driven by selfish motives (Ezekiel 34) and cunning (Jeremiah 10:21; 50:6), *"the good shepherd lays down His life for the sheep"* (John 10:11). This is precisely what Jesus, our Savior, did as it is recorded in the account of John 10:18. His selfless sacrifice describes His role as the Good Shepherd, who lays down His life for the sake of His sheep.

Being a wolf in sheep's clothing refers to the sin of pretending to be something we are not. It is the sin of hypocrisy, where we present ourselves as harmless and innocent, but inwardly, we are driven by selfish desires and motivations.

This sin is particularly dangerous because it can lead to deception and harm to others. When we pretend to be something we are not, we can gain the trust of others and then use that trust to manipulate and exploit them.

The Bible sounds a warning about the presence of false prophets who disguise themselves as harmless sheep, but inwardly are ravenous wolves (Matthew 7:15). This cautionary note is particularly relevant in these last days where Scripture foretells an increase in false prophets (Matthew 24:11). We must develop the ability to identify these wolves in sheep's clothing, not to foster a spirit of judgment or cynicism, but to protect ourselves and the vulnerable sheep within our communities.

As shepherds of God's flock, we have a sacred responsibility to guard the sheep, particularly the young and inexperienced believers. Our mandate is to emulate the wisdom of the serpent and the harmlessness of the dove, as Jesus instructs us in Matthew 10:16. Many believers have fallen prey to the cunning tactics of wolves
because they were too trusting and naive. While we should strive to maintain a positive and charitable attitude toward others, we must also cultivate wisdom and discernment to avoid being deceived.

The primary challenge in identifying wolves in sheep's clothing is that they often appear harmless and genuine from a distance. It is only when we draw closer that we can discern their true nature. This is where the danger lies, as we can easily become entrapped and hurt by their deceptive tactics. However, through personal experience and spiritual growth, we can develop the skills to recognize these wolves more quickly and effectively.

The Sin of Being a Sheep in Wolf's Clothing

In the previous explanation, we looked at the concept of wolves in sheep's clothing, where individuals disguise themselves as harmless and innocuous to trap or deceive, but in reality, they are predators seeking to devour and destroy. But what I want to talk about now is *the sheep in wolf's clothing*, an entirely different situation that we see all too often in the realm of faith-based recovery. This is another subtle and equally deceptive tactic employed by Satan, where he gives people false identities, making them appear as something they are not.

This phenomenon is what we refer to as a "sheep in wolf's clothing." It is a situation where an individual, who is internally a child of God, externally presents themselves as something entirely different, often working against the purposes of God.

Satan's strategy is to give people false identities, making them believe they are something they are not. He does this to confuse, deceive, and ultimately destroy. When we accept these false identities, we begin to live a life that is not authentic, and we start to work against our true nature and purpose.

The Sleeping Saint: A Sheep in Wolf's Clothing

When we hear the term "sleeping saint," our minds often wander to the biblical reference of a martyr who has died for the Gospel of Jesus Christ, only to rise again in judgment. However, there's another kind of "sleeping saint" - one who is still very much alive, but trapped in a facade of deception.

I'd like to share a powerful story of transformation that illustrates this concept. A young man, barely thirteen years old, found himself entangled in a web of drug abuse, including methamphetamine. His life was a mess, and it seemed like there was no escape. But then, something remarkable happened. He discovered Teen Challenge, a program that helped him break free from the chains of addiction. As he surrendered his life to the Lord, he experienced a profound transformation.

This young man was a perfect example of a "sheep in wolf's clothing." On the outside, he appeared tough and rebellious, intentionally projecting a false image to gain acceptance and credibility. But deep down, a sheep was waiting to be set free - a vulnerable, hurting, and lost soul crying out for help and redemption.

In the Bible, the story of Jacob is another fascinating example of a "sheep in wolf's clothing" in the person of Jacob. Jacob, whose name means "supplanter" or "deceiver," was a complex character who struggled with his identity and purpose.

On the outside, Jacob appeared to be a cunning and manipulative individual, always looking for ways to get ahead and gain an advantage over others. He was a master of deception, using his wit and cleverness to achieve his goals. This exterior persona was like a wolf's clothing, making him appear tough, resourceful, and willing to do whatever it took to succeed.

However, inwardly, Jacob was a sheep. He was a vulnerable, insecure, and fearful person who struggled with feelings of inadequacy and low self-esteem. Despite his tough exterior, Jacob was haunted by his past mistakes and struggled to find his place in the world.

One of the most significant events in Jacob's life was his encounter with God at Bethel. As he was fleeing from his brother Esau, Jacob had a profound experience with God, who appeared to him in a dream and promised to bless him and make him a great nation (Genesis 28:10-22).

This encounter marked a turning point in Jacob's life. He realized that his true identity was not as a wolf, but as a sheep. He started to understand that his strength and security came not from his cunning and manipulative ways, but from God Himself.

As Jacob continued on his journey, he faced many challenges and struggles. However, he also experienced a deepening of his faith and a growing sense of humility. He began to recognize that his true purpose was not to deceive and manipulate others, but to serve and bless them.

Eventually, Jacob's exterior persona began to reflect his inner transformation. He no longer felt the need to wear the wolf's clothing of deception and manipulation.
Instead, he was able to embrace his true identity as a sheep, humble, and dependent on God.

Jacob's story is a pointer that our true identity is not

defined by our exterior persona but by our inner character. We may try to wear the wolf's clothing of deception and manipulation, but ultimately, it is our inner sheep-like nature that will define us.

Jesus Himself spoke about this phenomenon in His priestly prayer in John 17. He expressed the will of the Father, stating that none should be lost. This mentality should be at the core of our being, driving us to reach out to those who are trapped in deception and darkness.

There are many "sleeping saints" among us who are concealed in plain sight, as this young man's story powerfully reminds us. Despite their wolf-like exterior, they are sheep just waiting to be released. Let's be on the lookout for these "sleeping saints" and assist them in realizing who they are in Christ as we adopt Jesus' mindset.

In the kingdom of God, identity is everything. Who we are and what we represent is crucial to our walk with God and our impact on the world around us. However, there is a sin that can creep into our lives and cause us to lose our true identity. This is the sin of being a wolf in sheep's clothing or a sheep in wolf's clothing.

As Jesus warned in Matthew 7:15, *"Beware of false prophets, who come to you in sheep's clothing but inwardly are ravenous wolves"* (AMPC). This passage highlights the danger of pretending to be something we're not. When we carry the wrong identity as believers, we can cause harm to ourselves and others.

To understand the nature of this sin, let's first examine the characteristics of sheep and wolves. Sheep are gentle, humble, and obedient creatures. They are followers, not leaders, and they are content to graze in the green pastures of God's presence. Sheep are also vulnerable and dependent on their shepherd for protection and care.

On the other hand, wolves are fierce, predatory, and destructive creatures. They are hunters, not followers; their instincts drive them to attack and devour their prey.

Wolves are also cunning and deceptive, using their sharp teeth and claws to manipulate and control others.

Now, let's compare the difference between a sheep and a wolf. A sheep is driven by a desire to follow and obey, while a wolf is driven by a desire to hunt and devour. A sheep is vulnerable and dependent, while a wolf is fierce and predatory. A sheep is gentle and humble, while a wolf is cunning and deceptive.

When we pretend to be something we're not, we can become like wolves in sheep's clothing. We may appear gentle and humble on the outside, but inwardly, we may be driven by a desire to manipulate and control others. We may use our sharp teeth and claws to attack and devour those around us rather than using our gifts and talents to serve and care for others.

For example, I recall the story of a brother who wore the appearance of a sheep and was so much celebrated for his lifestyle that looked like that of a sheep. However, he had successfully invaded the church and misled many sisters by promising to marry them. This brother was a classic example of a wolf in sheep's clothing. He appeared
to be gentle and humble on the outside, but inwardly, he was driven by a desire to manipulate and control others.

This brother's actions caused harm and destruction to many people in the church. He used his charm and deception to gain the trust of others, and then he used that trust to exploit and manipulate them. This is a classic example of the sin of being a wolf in sheep's clothing.

In contrast, a true sheep is driven by a desire to follow and obey God. They are gentle and humble, using their gifts and talents to serve and care for others. A true sheep is not driven by a desire to manipulate and control others but rather by a desire to love and serve others.

As believers, we must be careful not to pretend to be something we're not. We must be authentic and genuine in our walk with God and driven by a desire to love and serve others. We must not be like the brother who wore the appearance of a sheep but was inwardly a wolf. Instead, we must be like Jesus, the true Shepherd who laid down his life for the sheep.

As we explore the concept of wolves in sheep's clothing, it's essential to understand that these individuals can be found within the church. They may appear to be believers, but their actions and behaviors reveal their true nature.

The body of Christ has to war against satanic identity, and we need the help of God to overcome this struggle. As Paul wrote in Ephesians 6:12, "*For we do not wrestle against flesh and blood, but against the rulers, against the authorities, against the cosmic powers over this present darkness, against the spiritual forces of evil in the heavenly places*" (ESV).

We must be careful not to judge people by their actions, because we may miss that they genuinely love Jesus. Instead, we must pray that our true nature will rise to swallow and defeat that unwelcome intruder.

If we ignore sheep in wolf's clothing, we will be limited. God wants the world to see that we are sheep and that our wild side is a lion. However, when we wear wolf's clothing, we do not reflect our true identity as sheep.

Some of our children are genuine sheep, but every time we look at them, they are wearing wolf's clothing. This is because the devil is constantly seeking to stop us from attaining the best and the highest by putting us in the wrong clothing.

The wrong clothing that the devil seeks to put on us includes pride, laziness, foolishness, carelessness, shame, immorality, greed, selfishness, and self- centeredness. All these things are not ours, so we must never confuse foolishness for an

identity. This is where the sacrifice comes in – not to be who the enemy wants us
to be. We must truly check if we are wearing wolf's clothing and check all the identities of the wolves.

Wolves are some of the most loyal animals, the most intelligent animals. They are faithful, and their children go out to hunt for their parents. However, wolves also have a very bad side to them, and they look wrong because they hunt innocent sheep.

As believers, we must not exhibit these characteristics. We must not be loyal to the enemy but to God. We must not be intelligent in the ways of the world but in the ways of God. We must not be faithful to the enemy but to God.

Instead, we must be diligent, generous, loving, and growing in spiritual power, wisdom, and power. We must put on the new self, created after the likeness of God in true righteousness and holiness.

As Paul wrote in Ephesians 4:22-24, "*Put off your old self, which belongs to your former manner of life and is corrupt through deceitful desires, and be renewed in the spirit of your minds, and put on the new self, created after the likeness of God in true righteousness and holiness*" (ESV).

We must discard the old patched garment designed to keep people in bondage to sin. Instead, we must put on the new self, created after the likeness of God in true righteousness and holiness.

As Obadiah wrote in Obadiah 1:7, "*All the men who were allied with you have deceived you and have overcome you. Those who ate your bread have laid a snare under you; there is no understanding of it*" (NASB). We have no idea what happens when we come to the presence of God. The early church was powerful because they met daily. One week with no church makes one weak.

Therefore, we must never cool off or slow down, especially when we are going through things. We must not stay away from God or away from the house of God. Instead, we must continue to press in and excel in the ways and things of God.

We must continue to walk in the fullness of the spirit, constantly crying out for deliverance from the wolf's clothing that seeks to destroy us. As Paul wrote in 1 Corinthians 13:4, *"Love is patient and kind; love does not envy or boast; it is not arrogant or rude"* (ESV).

Let us be filled with love and continue to press in and excel in the ways and things of God. Let us put off the old man and put on the Lord Jesus, discarding the old patched garment designed to keep people in bondage to sin.

Let us be careful not to wear wolf's clothing, but instead, let us put on the new self, created after the likeness of God in true righteousness and holiness. Let us continue to walk in the fullness of the spirit, constantly crying out for deliverance from the wolf's clothing that seeks to destroy us. As Paul wrote in 1 Corinthians 13:4, *"Love is patient and kind; love does not envy or boast; it is not arrogant or rude"* (ESV).

Remember that the danger of a wolf in sheep's clothing is real and sheep in wolf's clothing is also real. Let us be vigilant and careful not to confuse our true identity as sheep with the wolf's clothing that the enemy is trying to put on us.

Let us continue to press in and excel in the ways and things of God. Let us put on the new self, created after the likeness of God in true righteousness and holiness. Let us be diligent, generous, loving, and growing in spiritual power, wisdom, and power.

As we move forward, let us remember that we are not alone in this battle. We have the help of God, and we have the support of our brothers and sisters in Christ. Let us stand together and fight against the wolves in sheep's clothing, knowing that we will emerge victorious in the end.

The Hidden Dangers of Wolves in Sheep's Clothing and Sheep in Wolf's Clothing

Identifying and recognizing wolves in sheep's clothing and

sheep in wolf's clothing can be a daunting task. It often requires proximity to recognize their true nature, and even then, it can be challenging to distinguish between the two. The danger of getting hurt and falling into the trap of the enemy is real, but by developing discernment and understanding the characteristics of these impostors, we can protect ourselves and our communities.

The Characteristics of Wolves in Sheep's Clothing

Wolves in sheep's clothing are masters of deception, using manipulation and lies to achieve their goals. They often present themselves as harmless and innocent, but in reality, they are predators seeking to devour and destroy. Here are some key characteristics they usually display as wolves in sheep's clothing:

An Issue with Spiritual Authority

Wolves in sheep's clothing often have a problem with spiritual authority, refusing to submit to legitimate leadership and guidance. Jesus Christ, the ultimate example of humility and submission, demonstrated a profound understanding of authority and the importance of being under authority. In John 15:19-20, He stated that He only did what He saw His Father in heaven doing, highlighting the significance of submitting to divine authority.

Real prophets, those who genuinely speak on behalf of God, are not rebellious people. They understand the concept of authority and recognize the importance of submitting to it. This is in stark contrast to wolves in sheep's clothing, who often have issues with spiritual authority.

In my encounters with wolves in sheep's clothing, I have consistently observed a lack of respect for spiritual authority. These individuals often exhibit a rebellious spirit, refusing to submit to legitimate leadership and guidance. This trait is a significant red flag, indicating that the person may be a wolf in sheep's clothing.

Rebellion against spiritual authority can have severe

consequences, leading to a breakdown in relationships, a lack of accountability, a diminished ability to receive guidance and correction, and then leading you away from the path to becoming the best, and the highest. It is essential to recognize the importance of submitting to spiritual authority and to be cautious of individuals who exhibit a rebellious spirit.

Manipulation and Control

They use manipulation and coercion to get what they want, often playing on people's emotions and vulnerabilities. Wolves in sheep's clothing can be incredibly deceptive, often presenting themselves as kind, gentle, and caring individuals. However, their true nature is revealed when they attempt to manipulate and control those around them. As long as they believe they can control you, they will continue to wear their mask of sweetness and innocence.

Wolves in sheep's clothing often operate under a spirit of tactful intimidation. They use subtle manipulation and coercion to get what they want, often making their victims feel guilty, ashamed, or fearful. This tactic can be incredibly effective, as it often goes undetected until it's too late.

It's essential to remember that manipulation and control are not characteristics of God's nature. God is a loving, gentle, and kind Father who desires a genuine relationship with His children. Anyone who claims to be sent by God cannot operate under a spirit of manipulation and control. This is a significant red flag, indicating that the person may be a wolf in sheep's clothing.

To protect yourself from the manipulation and control of wolves in sheep's clothing, it's crucial to develop a strong sense of discernment. You can protect yourself by

- *Familiarizing yourself with God's character, as described in the Bible. This will help you recognize when someone is operating under a spirit contrary to God's nature.*

- *Paying attention to inconsistencies in a person's words and actions. If they claim to be a Christian but exhibit manipulative and controlling behavior, it may be a sign that they are a wolf in sheep's clothing.*
- *Trusting your instincts. If you feel uncomfortable or sense that something is off about a person, trust your instincts. Don't ignore your feelings or try to rationalize them away.*
- *Surrounding yourself with trusted advisors by having a support system of trusted friends, family, or mentors can help you stay safe from manipulation and control. Don't be afraid to seek advice or guidance from those you trust.*

By being aware of the deceptive nature of wolves in sheep's clothing and developing a strong sense of discernment, you can protect yourself from manipulation and control. Remember, God is a loving and gentle Father who desires a genuine relationship with His children. Anyone who claims to be sent by God cannot operate under a spirit of manipulation and control.

Lack of Spiritual Fruit

Wolves in sheep's clothing often lack genuine spiritual fruit, such as peace, patience, gentleness, and self-control.

The Bible emphasizes the importance of examining the spiritual fruit in others to determine their true nature. Jesus taught that a tree is recognized by its fruit and that a good tree cannot bear bad fruit, nor can a bad tree bear good fruit (Matthew 7:17-18). When it comes to wolves in sheep's clothing, there is often rotten fruit in their lives that can be observed if we know what to look for.

So, what does rotten fruit look like in the life of a wolf in sheep's clothing?

- **Lack of peace**: *Wolves in sheep's clothing often*

create chaos and stir up conflict wherever they go. They may be prone to anger, irritability, and impatience.

- **Impatience and impulsiveness**: They may act impulsively, making decisions without considering the consequences or seeking guidance from others.
- **Lack of gentleness**: Wolves in sheep's clothing may be harsh, critical, and unkind in their words and actions. They may belittle or mock others, using their words to wound and destroy.
- **Lack of self-control**: They may struggle with addictions, compulsions, or other behaviors that demonstrate a lack of self-control. They may be prone to outbursts of anger, lust, or other sinful behaviors.
- **Constant stirring up of chaos**: Wolves in sheep's clothing often create drama and conflict wherever they go. They may stir up trouble, gossip, or slander, causing division and strife among others.

So, how can we check the spiritual fruit in others to determine if they are wolves in sheep's clothing?

- **Observe their behavior**: Watch how they interact with others, especially in challenging situations. Do they respond with patience, kindness, and compassion, or do they become angry, defensive, or aggressive?
- **Examine their words**: Listen to what they say, especially when they are speaking about others or difficult topics. Do their words build up and encourage, or do they tear down and destroy?
- **Look for consistency**: Check if their words and actions are consistent with each other. Do they practice what they preach, or do they say one thing but do another?

- **Check for the fruit of the Spirit**: *Look for evidence of the fruit of the Spirit in their lives, such as love, joy, peace, patience, kindness, goodness, faithfulness, gentleness, and self-control (Galatians 5:22-23). Are these characteristics present in their lives, or are they lacking?*
- **Inconsistent behavior**: *They may exhibit inconsistent behavior, such as being friendly and charming in public but revealing their true nature in private.*
- **History of manipulation and control**: *Wolves in sheep's clothing often have a history of manipulating and controlling others, using tactics such as guilt, shame, and fear to achieve their goals.*

The Characteristics of Sheep in Wolf's Clothing

Sheep in wolf's clothing, on the other hand, are individuals who, despite being children of God, present themselves in a way that is contrary to their true nature. They often experience internal conflict, feeling torn between their genuine identity and the false persona they have assumed. Here are some key characteristics of sheep in wolf's clothing:

Internal Conflict

Sheep in wolf's clothing often struggle with feelings of guilt, shame, and anxiety, as they try to reconcile their true identity with their false persona. A sheep in wolf's clothing is an individual who, despite being a child of God, presents themselves in a way that is contrary to their true nature. This can lead to a profound sense of internal conflict, as the person struggles to reconcile their genuine identity with the false persona they have assumed.

The internal conflict experienced by a sheep in wolf's clothing can stem from various factors, like;

- **Fear and insecurity**: *The person may feel pressure to conform to certain expectations or standards, leading them to hide their true self and present a false image.*
- **Lack of self-awareness**: *They may not have a clear understanding of their own thoughts, feelings, and motivations, making it difficult for them to reconcile their true identity with their false persona.*
- **External influences**: *The person may be surrounded by people who encourage or reinforce their false identity, making it challenging for them to break free from the internal conflict.*

These internal conflicts experienced by a sheep in wolf's clothing can have severe consequences that hinders the individual from becoming the best and the highest. The consequences may include:

- **Emotional turmoil**: *The person may experience intense emotional pain, anxiety, and depression as they struggle to reconcile their true identity with their false persona.*
- **Spiritual stagnation**: *The internal conflict can hinder the person's spiritual growth and development, making it challenging for them to deepen their relationship with God.*
- **Damaged relationships**: *The false persona presented by the sheep in wolf's clothing can lead to damaged relationships with others, as they may struggle to form genuine connections with people.*

External Deception

Wolves in sheep's clothing are masters of deception, presenting themselves to the world in a way that is contrary to their true nature. They use manipulation and deception to achieve their goals, often leaving a trail of destruction and chaos in their wake.

Wolves in sheep's clothing are skilled at deceiving others, using various tactics to manipulate and control those around them. Some common deceptive tactics used by wolves in sheep's clothing include:

- *Pretenses: They may present themselves as something they are not, such as a spiritual leader, a trusted friend, or a confidant.*
- *Manipulative language: Wolves in sheep's clothing may use language that is designed to manipulate and control others, such as guilt-tripping, gaslighting, or emotional blackmail.*
- *Emotional manipulation: They may use emotional manipulation to control and influence others, such as playing on people's emotions, using flattery, or making false promises.*
- *Hidden agendas: Wolves in sheep's clothing often have hidden agendas, using deception and manipulation to achieve their goals without revealing their true intentions.*

We can unmask the truth and reveal the deception of wolves in sheep's clothing, by simply;

- *Developing a discerning spirit, being able to distinguish between truth and deception.*
- *Paying attention to inconsistencies in a person's words and actions, as this can be a sign of deception.*
- *Examining the fruit of a person's life, looking for evidence of spiritual growth, kindness, compassion, and empathy.*
- *Surrounding yourself with wise and discerning individuals who can offer guidance and support in navigating complex relationships.*

By being aware of the deceptive tactics used by wolves in sheep's clothing and developing a discerning spirit, we can unmask the truth and avoid being deceived by these impostors.

Working against God's Purposes

The fact that a sheep in wolf's clothing frequently finds oneself acting contrary to God's will is a profound challenge. This can happen intentionally or inadvertently, underscoring the intricate and subtle character of spiritual deception.

Spiritual deception can be a subtle and insidious force, often masquerading as truth or righteousness. A sheep in wolf's clothing may be deceived into believing that they are doing God's work when in reality they are perpetuating harm and darkness. This can occur through:

- **Misinterpretation of scripture**: *A sheep in wolf's clothing may misinterpret or distort biblical teachings to justify their actions, which are contrary to God's purposes.*
- **Blind spots and biases**: *They may have blind spots or biases that prevent them from seeing the harm they are causing, or from recognizing the true nature of their actions.*
- **Influence of external factors**: *A sheep in wolf's clothing may be influenced by external factors, such as cultural or societal pressures, that lead them to work against God's purposes.*

When a sheep in wolf's clothing works against God's purposes, either knowingly or unknowingly, it can have severe consequences, which include:

- **Harm to others**: *Their actions may cause harm to others, either directly or indirectly, perpetuating darkness and suffering.*
- **Damage to their spiritual growth**: *Working against God's purposes can hinder a sheep in wolf's clothing's spiritual growth and development, leading to stagnation and spiritual decay.*
- **Disruption of God's plans**: *Their actions may disrupt God's plans and purposes, either in their*

own life or in the lives of others.

Wolves In Sheep's Clothing Can Be Gifted:

Just because someone has spiritual gifts does not mean they are heaven-sent. Many times, people are mistaken by these individuals just because they were gifted or because a 'prophetic word' seemed accurate.

In the pursuit of building and growing the church and raising people who will become the best and highest, it's essential to exercise discernment when evaluating individuals with spiritual gifts. While gifts such as prophecy, healing, and teaching are valuable assets to the body of Christ, they do not automatically qualify someone for leadership or ministry roles.

It's crucial to recognize that spiritual gifts can be counterfeited or misused by individuals who are not genuinely sent by God. The Bible warns us about false prophets and teachers who can perform signs and wonders, but are serving their interests or promoting false doctrine (Matthew 24:24, 2 Peter 2:1-3).

When evaluating individuals with spiritual gifts, it's essential to look beyond their gifts and examine their character and fruit. Do they demonstrate a lifestyle of humility, integrity, and obedience to God's Word? Are they accountable to spiritual authority and willing to submit to correction and guidance?

If you are a pastor or a church leader reading this book, please exercise caution when considering individuals with spiritual gifts for leadership or ministry roles. While their gifts may be impressive, it's crucial to evaluate their character, fruit, and lifestyle before placing them in positions of influence.

Failing to exercise discernment when evaluating

individuals with spiritual gifts can have severe consequences, and some of these consequences include:

- **Damage to the flock**: *Allowing individuals with false or misused gifts to minister to the flock can lead to spiritual damage, confusion, and harm.*
- **Erosion of trust**: *When church leaders fail to discern the motives and character of individuals with spiritual gifts, it can erode trust within the congregation and damage the reputation of the church.*
- **Promotion of false doctrine**: *Allowing individuals with false or misused gifts to teach or preach can lead to the promotion of false doctrine, which can have far- reaching and devastating consequences.*

While spiritual gifts are essential to the functioning of the body of Christ, they must be evaluated in conjunction with an individual's character, fruit, and lifestyle. Church leaders must exercise discernment and caution when considering individuals with spiritual gifts for leadership or ministry roles, lest they inadvertently promote false doctrine or harm the flock.

Wolves didn't always start out being wolves. Often, they are gifted individuals who just got lost somewhere along the way. They may have experienced father fractures, never quite healed, and let the idea of success get in the way of morality.

The Bible is very clear that we need to learn how to check the spiritual fruit in others. Are they people of peace, patience, gentleness, and self-control? Do they consistently stir up chaos or set you on edge?

Identifying and recognizing wolves in sheep's clothing and sheep in wolf's clothing is crucial for our spiritual well-being, and protection of our communities and in preparing us to become the best and the highest. By understanding the characteristics of these impostors and developing discernment, we can avoid the dangers of the enemy and stay safe in the flock. Remember, the enemy is not the person, but the devil to which the person has given a foothold in their life. This is a spiritual matter that requires spiritual discernment and wisdom.

Overcoming the Sin of Being a Wolf in Sheep's Clothing or a Sheep in Wolf's Clothing

The sin of being a wolf in sheep's clothing or a sheep in wolf's clothing is a pervasive and destructive issue that can have far-reaching consequences for individuals, communities, and the body of Christ as a whole. To overcome this sin, it is essential to embark on a journey of self-discovery and transformation, marked by a commitment to honesty, humility, and spiritual growth.

Before we can overcome the sin of being a wolf in sheep's clothing or a sheep in wolf's clothing, we must first understand the nature of wolves which I have already elaborated on in the earlier part of this chapter. Wolves are known for their loyalty, intelligence, and faithfulness, but they also have a darker side, marked by a predatory instinct that drives them to hunt and devour innocent sheep.

To overcome the sin of being a wolf in sheep's clothing, we must be able to recognize the characteristics of a wolf in sheep's clothing which we have discussed in this chapter.

To overcome the sin of being a wolf in sheep's clothing or a sheep in wolf's clothing, it is essential to engage in regular self-reflection and examination. This involves asking yourself questions such as:

- *Am I diligent and hardworking, or do I rely on manipulation and deception to achieve my goals?*
- *Am I generous and willing to share my resources with others, or do I use my wealth and influence to control and manipulate those around me?*

- *Am I loving and compassionate towards others, or do I use people for my gain and exploit them for my benefit?*
- *Am I growing in spiritual power, wisdom, and knowledge, or do I rely on my natural talents and abilities to achieve my goals?*

To overcome the sin of being a wolf in sheep's clothing or a sheep in wolf's clothing, we must be willing to undergo a process of transformation. This process involves:

- *Putting off the old man: We must put off the old man, with its sinful nature and tendencies, and put on the new man, created in the image of God (Ephesians 4:22-24).*
- *Discarding the old patched garment: We must discard the old patched garment, designed to keep us in bondage to sin, and put on the Lord Jesus Christ, who sets us free from the power of sin (Romans 13:14).*
- *Walking in the fullness of the Spirit: We must walk in the fullness of the Spirit, being filled with the love, joy, peace, patience, kindness, goodness, faithfulness, gentleness, and self-control that is the fruit of the Spirit (Galatians 5:22-23).*

Finally, overcoming the sin of being a wolf in sheep's clothing or a sheep in wolf's clothing requires a deep commitment to honesty, humility, and spiritual growth. By engaging in regular self-reflection and examination, putting off the old man and putting on the new man, discarding the old patched garment and putting on the Lord Jesus Christ, and walking in the fullness of the Spirit, we can overcome this sin, live a life that is pleasing to God and become the best and highest.

CHAPTER SIX

The Sin of Ignoring, Neglecting, or Avoiding the Call to Sacrificial Living to Advancing God's Kingdom

"I am the Good Shepherd. The Good Shepherd puts the sheep before himself, sacrifices himself if necessary. A hired man is not a real shepherd. He doesn't own the sheep, and they don't matter to him. When a wolf shows up, he runs for it, leaving the sheep to fend for themselves. He's only in it for the money. The sheep don't matter to him. I am the Good Shepherd. I know my own sheep and my own sheep know me. In the same way, the Father knows me and I know the Father. I put the sheep before myself, sacrificing myself if necessary. You need to know that I have other sheep in other folds, and I will bring them to join this flock, so they will all be together. Then I will be their Shepherd, and they will all be in my care. The Father loves me because I freely lay down my life. And so I am free to take it up again. No one takes it from me. I lay it down of my own free will. I have the right to lay it down, and I have the right to take it up again. I received this authority from my Father." **John 10:11-18 MSG**

In John 10:11-18 MSG, Jesus presents Himself as the Good Shepherd, who puts the sheep before Himself and sacrifices, illustrating sacrificial living, which is a fundamental aspect of advancing God's kingdom. Carefully reading this passage, we will discover the importance of sacrificial living and how Jesus' example can inspire and empower us to live a life of sacrifice and service to others if we want to become the best and highest.

Jesus who is the Good Shepherd and a model of sacrificial living described Himself as One who is willing to lay down His life for the sheep. His comments about laying down his life express the depth of His love and commitment to those He has been called to serve. The Good Shepherd is not just a title; it is a way of life that is characterized by sacrifice, service, and a deep love for others.

As we reflect on Jesus' words, we are reminded that sacrificial living is not just about giving up things we value or enjoy; it is about putting the needs of others before our own. It is about being willing to lay down our lives, our comfort, and our security for the sake of advancing God's kingdom. This is the example that Jesus sets for us, and it is an example that we must follow if we are to truly live a life of sacrifice and service to others.

Throughout Jesus' earthly ministry, He demonstrated the power of sacrificial living. He gave up the comforts of heaven to come to earth, to live among us, and to ultimately give His life for our salvation. He spent His days serving others, healing the sick, feeding the hungry, and preaching the gospel to those who were lost. He was a
true servant-leader, who put the needs of others before His own, and who was willing to make the ultimate sacrifice for the sake of advancing God's kingdom.

Sacrificial living is essential for advancing God's kingdom. When we are willing to put the needs of others before our own, we create an environment in which God's kingdom can flourish. We demonstrate the love and character of God to a world that is in desperate need of hope and redemption.

As we live a life of sacrifice and service to others, we also create opportunities for others to experience the love and power of God. We become ambassadors for Christ, representing Him to a world that does not know Him. We become instruments of God's grace and mercy, extending His love and compassion to those who are in need.

As we journey through the Christian life, we are constantly faced with choices that determine our level of commitment to God's kingdom. One of the most critical decisions we can make is whether to embrace a life of sacrificial living, which is essential for advancing God's kingdom and glorifying Him in the way He desires.

In John 10:11-18 (MSG), Jesus teaches us that the authority to lead and serve in God's kingdom is directly tied to our willingness to live sacrificially. The Good Shepherd lays down His life for His sheep, demonstrating the ultimate act of sacrificial love. As we follow in Jesus' footsteps, we must be willing to surrender our interests, desires, and comforts for the sake of advancing God's kingdom.

Unfortunately, many Christians neglect or avoid the call to sacrificial living, often due to fear, complacency, or a lack of understanding about the importance of this lifestyle. However, the consequences of neglecting sacrificial living are severe. As Jesus taught, "If anyone wants to follow in my footsteps, he must deny himself, pick up his cross, and start following me" (Matthew 16:24, TPT). Those who refuse to take up their cross and follow Jesus will not experience the fullness of spiritual power and authority that comes with sacrificial living.

As believers, church workers, and leaders, we are called to a life of sacrificial living, dedicated to advancing God's kingdom and fulfilling His purposes on earth. This call is not optional, but rather a fundamental aspect of our faith and discipleship. We are expected to live a life that is characterized by sacrifice, service, and a deep commitment to the advancement of God's kingdom.

To live a life of sacrificial living, we must be actively involved in advancing God's kingdom. This involves using our resources, talents, and time to further the kingdom and fulfill

God's purposes. We must be willing to roll up our sleeves and get involved in the work of the kingdom, whether it's through evangelism, discipleship, serving the poor, or other forms of ministry.

As we seek to live a life of sacrificial living and advance God's kingdom, we must be careful to avoid distractions and wrong teachings that can take our hearts away from kingdom business. We must be discerning and wise, able to distinguish between true and false teachings, and avoid anything that would hinder our effectiveness in advancing the kingdom.

One of the most significant distractions and wrong teachings that we must avoid is the idea that we should withdraw our financial commitments to advancing God's kingdom. This teaching is not only unbiblical, but it is also detrimental to the advancement of the kingdom. As believers, we are called to be generous and sacrificial in our giving, using our financial resources to further the kingdom and fulfill God's purposes.

"Do not store up for yourselves treasures on earth, where moths and vermin destroy, and where thieves break in and steal. But store up for yourselves treasures in heaven, where moths and vermin do not destroy, and where thieves do not break in and steal.

For where your treasure is, there your heart will be also."
Matthew 6:19-21

Sacrificial living is not a one-time event, but a consistent lifestyle of obedience to God's will. As we surrender our lives to God, we must be willing to make sacrifices on a daily basis, whether it's giving up our time, resources, or comfort for the sake of advancing God's kingdom. This consistent sacrificial obedience is what sets apart those who are truly committed to following Jesus and advancing His kingdom.

The Power of Sacrificial Living

As we embark on a journey of sacrificial living, we can expect to experience a profound transformation in our lives. We will begin to see the world through God's eyes, and our hearts will be filled with a deep sense of compassion, love, and concern for others. We will be empowered to live a life that is pleasing to God, and our sacrifices will be used by God to bring about breakthroughs, miracles, and transformations in our lives and the lives of those around us.

One of the greatest obstacles to sacrificial living is fear. Fear of failure, fear of losses, fear of the unknown. However, as we surrender our lives to God, we must be willing to overcome these fears and trust in God's sovereignty and goodness. We must remember that our sacrifices are not in vain, but are used by God to bring about a greater good. As we press on in our journey of sacrificial living, we will begin to see the fruit of our labor and our hearts will be filled with joy, peace, and a deep sense of fulfillment.

The Call to Be a Special Vessel

As we consider the call to sacrificial living, we must also recognize the importance of being a special vessel, set apart for God's use. Just as the Navy SEALs are an elite group of warriors, trained to carry out special operations, so too must we be willing to be trained and equipped by God for the special task of advancing His kingdom. We must be willing to surrender our lives, our comfort, and our security for the sake of the gospel, and trust in God's power and provision to carry us through.

The Choice is Ours

As we stand at the crossroads of our journey, we are faced with a critical choice. Will we choose to embrace a life of sacrificial living, or will we opt for a more comfortable, convenient Christianity? The choice is ours, but we must remember that our decision will have eternal consequences. One day, time will be no more, and we will cross into eternity, where we will live with the reality of the choices we made here on earth.

God desires to give us the best of everything, to bestow upon us the highest honors, and to lavish us with extravagant rewards. However, to experience this level of blessing and favor, we must be willing to live a sacrificial life in God's kingdom business.

This means giving the best of our service in God's house, serving with a heart of love, humility, and obedience. We must not serve like a wolf in sheep's clothing or like a sheep in wolf's clothing, but rather with a genuine and sincere heart.

Giving is an essential aspect of living a sacrificial life in God's kingdom. We must give where we need to give, being committed to tithing and offering our resources to God as an expression of our love for Him. We must not give grudgingly or with a sense of obligation, but rather with a cheerful and willing heart.

As we strive to live a sacrificial life in God's kingdom, we must be careful to avoid

living a careless, wicked, and unprofitable life. Don't be an unprofitable servant, put what God has given to you into business and make a profit with it, so you can use it to make an impact in the lives of others, and raise business that would be used to finance Kingdom business. Take a risk, because it is risky not to take a risk. The master rejected the unprofitable servant because he didn't want to take a risk. Be intentional and purposeful in your actions, words, and decisions, and seek to honor God in all that we do.

> *"Then the servant who had received the one bag of silver came forward and said, 'Master, I knew you were a hard man, harvesting crops you didn't plant and gathering crops you didn't cultivate. I was afraid I would lose your money, so I hid it in the ground. See, here is your money back. But the master replied, 'You wicked and lazy servant! If you knew I harvested crops I didn't plant and gathered crops I didn't cultivate, you should have put my money on deposit with the bankers, or at least invested it so I could have earned some interest on it.*

Take the bag of silver away from him,' the master said, 'and give it to the servant who has the ten bags of silver. To those who use well what they are given, even more will be given, and they will have an abundance. But from those who do nothing, even what little they have will be taken away.'"
Matthew 25:28-30 (NLT)

As we seek to live a sacrificial life in God's kingdom, we must follow in the footsteps of Jesus Christ, who gave Himself sacrificially for the sake of humanity. We must be willing to deny ourselves, take up our cross, and follow Jesus, no matter where He may lead.

Ignoring, Neglecting, or Avoiding the Call to Sacrificial Living: A Hindrance to Glorifying God

As believers, we are called to live a life of sacrificial living, denying ourselves, taking up our cross, and following Jesus (Matthew 16:24). However, many believers ignore, neglect, or avoid this call, hindering their ability to glorify God the way He wants to be glorified.

One of the primary ways believers ignore, neglect, or avoid the call to sacrificial living is by prioritizing their interests and desires above God's. This can manifest in various ways, such as pursuing wealth, status, and power, rather than seeking to advance God's kingdom (1 Timothy 6:10).

Another way believers ignore, neglect, or avoid the call to sacrificial living is by being unwilling to surrender their lives to God. This can involve holding onto personal ambitions, desires, and dreams, rather than submitting them to God's will and purpose (Romans 12:1-2).

Some believers also ignore, neglect, or avoid the call to sacrificial living by being fearful of the costs and consequences of following Jesus. This can involve being afraid of persecution, rejection, or hardship, rather than trusting in God's sovereignty and provision (Matthew 10:28-33).

Additionally, believers may ignore, neglect, or avoid the

call to sacrificial living by being distracted by the world and its allurements. This can involve being consumed by materialism, entertainment, and other worldly pursuits, rather than focusing on eternal things and seeking to advance God's kingdom (1 John 2:15-17).

Some believers also ignore, neglect, or avoid the call to sacrificial living by being influenced by false teachings and doctrines that emphasize personal gain and prosperity rather than sacrifice and service. This can involve being taught that God's primary concern is to bless and prosper us, rather than to use us to advance His kingdom and glorify Himself (2 Timothy 4:3-4).

Furthermore, believers may ignore, neglect, or avoid the call to sacrificial living by being unwilling to confront and surrender their sin and selfishness. This can involve being in denial about the state of their heart and life, rather than acknowledging and confessing their sin and seeking to live a life of obedience and surrender to God (1 John 1:8-10).

Another way believers ignore, neglect, or avoid the call to sacrificial living is by being disconnected from the body of Christ and lacking accountability and support. This can involve being isolated and individualistic in their faith, rather than being part of a community of believers who can encourage, support, and challenge them to live a life of sacrifice and service (Hebrews 10:24-25).

Some believers also ignore, neglect, or avoid the call to sacrificial living by being focused on their spiritual growth and development, rather than seeking to serve and bless others. This can involve being self-centered and individualistic in their faith, rather than being outward-focused and seeking to advance God's kingdom (Philippians 2:3-4).

Additionally, believers may ignore, neglect, or avoid the call to sacrificial living by being unaware of or unresponsive to the needs and opportunities around them. This can involve being oblivious to the spiritual and physical needs of others, rather than being aware and responsive to the opportunities to serve and bless others (Proverbs 3:27-28).

Furthermore, believers may ignore, neglect, or avoid the call to sacrificial living by being unwilling to take risks and step out in faith. This can involve being fearful of uncertainty and unpredictability, rather than trusting in God's sovereignty and provision (Hebrews 11:6).

Some believers also ignore, neglect, or avoid the call to sacrificial living by being overly focused on their comfort and security. This can involve being unwilling to sacrifice their comfort and security for the sake of advancing God's kingdom, rather than being willing to take up their cross and follow Jesus (Matthew 10:38-39).

Another way believers ignore, neglect, or avoid the call to sacrificial living is by being influenced by the values and priorities of the world. This can involve being conformed to the pattern of the world, rather than being transformed by the renewing of their mind and seeking to live a life that is pleasing to God (Romans 12:2).

Moreover, believers may ignore, neglect, or avoid the call to sacrificial living by being lacking in discernment and wisdom. This can involve being unable to distinguish
between good and evil, right and wrong, and being unaware of the devices and strategies of the enemy (Hebrews 5:14).

Some believers also ignore, neglect, or avoid the call to sacrificial living by being lazy and complacent. This can involve being unwilling to put in the effort and hard work required to live a life of sacrifice and service, and being content with a mediocre and lukewarm faith (Revelation 3:15-17).

Additionally, believers may ignore, neglect, or avoid the call to sacrificial living by being fearful of what others may think or say. This can involve being concerned about their reputation and image, rather than being willing to take a stand for Christ and live a life that is pleasing to Him

(Galatians 1:10).

Moreover, believers may ignore, neglect, or avoid the call to sacrificial living by being unaware of or unresponsive to the needs of the lost and the hurting. This can involve being oblivious to the spiritual and physical needs of others, rather than being aware and responsive to the opportunities to serve and bless others (Proverbs 3:27-28).

Additionally, believers may ignore, neglect, or avoid the call to sacrificial living by being unwilling to forgive and let go of past hurts and offenses. This can involve being held back by bitterness and unforgiveness, rather than being willing to forgive and let go, and move forward in their walk with God (Matthew 6:14-15).

Furthermore, believers may ignore, neglect, or avoid the call to sacrificial living by being influenced by the spirit of entitlement. This can involve being consumed by a sense of entitlement and expectation, rather than being willing to humble themselves and serve others (Philippians 2:5-8).

Some believers also ignore, neglect, or avoid the call to sacrificial living by being unaware of or unresponsive to the promptings of the Holy Spirit. This can involve being oblivious to the gentle nudges and promptings of the Holy Spirit, rather than being aware and responsive to His leading and guidance (John 16:13).

Moreover, believers may ignore, neglect, or avoid the call to sacrificial living by being focused on their strength and abilities, rather than relying on God's power and provision. This can involve being self-sufficient and independent, rather than being willing to depend on God and trust in His sovereignty (2 Corinthians 12:9-10).

The Call to Sacrificial Living

The call to sacrificial living is a call to die to ourselves and live for Christ. It is a call to surrender our lives, our desires, and our ambitions to God, and to seek to live a life that is pleasing to Him.

As believers, we are called to live a life of sacrifice and service, using our gifts, talents, and resources to advance God's kingdom and glorify Him. We are called to be willing to take risks, step out in faith, and trust in God's sovereignty and provision.

The call to sacrificial living is not a call to a life of ease and comfort, but rather a call to a life of sacrifice and service. It is a call to die to ourselves and live for Christ, to surrender our lives to God, and to seek to live a life that is pleasing to Him.

The Rewards of Sacrificial Living

The rewards of sacrificial living are numerous and eternal. As believers, when we live a life of sacrifice and service, we can expect to experience a deeper and more intimate relationship with God. We can expect to experience a sense of purpose and fulfillment, knowing that we are living a life that is pleasing to God.

We can also expect to experience the joy and satisfaction of seeing lives changed and transformed through our service and ministry. We can expect to experience the blessing of God's provision and supply, as we trust in His sovereignty and provision.

Furthermore, as believers, when we live a life of sacrifice and service, we can expect to experience the reward of eternal life and the promise of heaven. We can expect to hear the words of Jesus, *"Well done, good and faithful servant. You have been faithful over a little; I will set you over much. Enter into the joy of your master"* (Matthew 25:21).

The Consequences of Ignoring the Call to Sacrificial Living

On the other hand, when believers ignore, neglect, or avoid the call to sacrificial living, they can expect to experience a range of negative consequences. They can expect to experience a sense of emptiness and purposelessness, knowing that they are not living a life that is pleasing to God and living the life that God wants for every believer, the life we are all called to live – becoming the best and the highest.

They can also expect to experience the consequences of a life of self-centeredness and individualism, rather than a life of sacrifice and service. They can expect to experience the consequences of a life that is focused on temporal and earthly things, rather than eternal and heavenly things.

Furthermore, when believers ignore, neglect, or avoid the call to sacrificial living, they can expect to experience the judgment and discipline of God. They can expect to hear the words of Jesus, *"I never knew you; depart from Me, you who practice lawlessness"* (Matthew 7:23).

The call to sacrificial living is a call to all believers, regardless of their background, culture, or socioeconomic status. It is a call to die to ourselves and live for Christ, to surrender our lives to God, and to seek to live a life that is pleasing to Him.

As believers, we must recognize that the call to sacrificial living is not optional, but rather it is a necessary part of our walk with God. We must be willing to surrender our lives, our desires, and our ambitions to God, and to seek to live a life that is pleasing to Him.

The Sin of Ignoring, Neglecting, or Avoiding the Call to Sacrificial Living to Advance God's Kingdom and glorifying God is a serious offense that hinders the advancement of God's kingdom. It refers to the intentional or unintentional refusal to surrender one's life, desires, and ambitions to God, thereby hindering the advancement of His kingdom. This sin involves prioritizing personal interests and desires above God's will and purpose, leading to a life of self-centeredness, individualism, and spiritual stagnation.

As believers, we must recognize the gravity of this sin and take steps to overcome it. We must be willing to surrender our lives, desires, and ambitions to God, and seek to live a life that is pleasing to Him.

Overcoming The Sin of Ignoring, Neglecting, or Avoiding the Call to Sacrificial Living

So, how can we overcome The Sin of Ignoring, Neglecting, or Avoiding the Call to Sacrificial Living?

Surrender to God

The first step to overcoming this sin is to surrender our lives, desires, and ambitions to God. We must be willing to let go of our plans and desires and seek to live a life that is pleasing to Him.

In Genesis 22:1-14, Abraham was called by God to sacrifice his only son, Isaac, as a test of his faith and obedience. Abraham's response to God's call is a remarkable example of surrender to God. Although Isaac was his only son, and the promise of God's covenant was tied to him, Abraham was willing to let go of his plans and desires and surrender to God's will.

In Genesis 22:2, God says to Abraham, "*Take now your son, your only son Isaac, whom you love, and go to the land of Moriah, and offer him there as a burnt offering on one of the mountains of which I shall tell you.*" Abraham's response is recorded in Genesis 22:3, "*So Abraham rose early in the morning and saddled his donkey, and took two of his young men with him, and Isaac his son; and he split the wood for the burnt offering, and arose and went to the place of which God had told him.*"

Abraham's surrender to God is evident in his willingness to obey God's command, even when it seemed to go against his plans and desires. He was willing to let go of his attachment to Isaac and surrender to God's will, trusting that God would provide and fulfill His promises.

As believers, we can learn from Abraham's example of surrender to God. We must be willing to let go of our plans and desires and surrender to God's will, trusting that He has our best interests at heart and that His plans are always good and perfect.

Seek God's Will and Purpose

We must seek to understand God's will and purpose for our lives and seek to align our lives with His plans. This involves reading and studying God's Word, seeking guidance from the Holy Spirit, seeking counsel from mature believers, and considering seeking prophetic guidance from genuine prophets.

A powerful example of seeking God's will and purpose can be seen in the life of David, as recorded in 1 Samuel 23:1-12. David was facing a difficult decision, as he was being pursued by King Saul and needed to know whether to attack the Philistines who were attacking the town of Keilah.

David's response to this situation is a remarkable example of seeking God's will and purpose. In 1 Samuel 23:2, it is recorded that *"David inquired of the Lord, saying, 'Shall I go and attack these Philistines?' And the Lord said to David, 'Go and attack the Philistines, and save Keilah.'"* David sought guidance from the Lord, and the Lord provided him with clear direction.

However, David did not stop there. He continued to seek God's will and purpose, as recorded in 1 Samuel 23:4, *"Then David inquired of the Lord once again. And the Lord answered him and said, 'Arise, go down to Keilah, for I will deliver the Philistines into your hand.'"* David sought confirmation from the Lord, and the Lord provided him with assurance.

David's example shows us the importance of seeking God's will and purpose in our lives. We must be willing to seek guidance from the Lord, to seek confirmation from Him, and to trust in His sovereignty and direction for our lives.

Prioritize God's Kingdom

We must prioritize God's kingdom above our interests and desires. This involves being willing to make sacrifices and put the needs of others before our own. A very good example of prioritizing God's kingdom can be seen in the life of the apostle Paul, recorded in Philippians 3:1-14. Paul was a zealous and ambitious man, who had a strong desire to serve God and advance His kingdom.

However, Paul's ambition and desire for success were not focused on his interests and desires, but rather on advancing God's kingdom. In Philippians 3:7-8, Paul writes, "*But whatever things were gain to me, those things I have counted as loss for the sake of Christ. More than that, I count all things to be loss in view of the surpassing value of knowing Christ Jesus my Lord, for whom I have suffered the loss of all things, and count them but rubbish so that I may gain Christ.*"

Paul's example shows us the importance of prioritizing God's kingdom above our interests and desires. He was willing to make sacrifices and put the needs of others before his own, in order to advance God's kingdom.

Live a Life of Sacrificial Living

We must be willing to live a life of sacrificial living, using our gifts, talents, and resources to advance God's kingdom. This involves being willing to take risks, step out in faith, and trust in God's sovereignty and provision. A perfect example of living a life of sacrificial living can be seen in the life of the apostle Paul, as recorded in 2 Corinthians 11:23-28. Paul was a missionary and evangelist who traveled extensively throughout the Mediterranean world, preaching the gospel and establishing churches.

Paul's ministry was marked by incredible sacrifice and hardship. In 2 Corinthians 11:23- 28, he writes, "*Are they servants of Christ?—I speak as if insane—I more so; in far more labors, in far more imprisonments, beaten times without number, often in danger of death. Five times I received from the Jews thirty-nine lashes. Three times I was beaten with rods, once I was stoned, three times I was shipwrecked, a night and a day I have spent in the deep. I have been on frequent journeys, in dangers from rivers, dangers from robbers, dangers from my countrymen, dangers from the Gentiles, dangers in the city, dangers in the wilderness, dangers on the sea, dangers among false brethren; I have been in labor and hardship, through many sleepless nights, in hunger and thirst, often without food, in cold and exposure."*

Paul's example shows us the importance of living a life of sacrificial living, using our gifts, talents, and resources to advance God's kingdom. He was willing to take risks, step out in faith, and trust in God's sovereignty and provision, even amid incredible hardship and sacrifice.

Seek Accountability and Support

We must seek accountability and support from other believers, who can encourage, support, and challenge us to live a life of sacrificial living. Seeking accountability and support can be seen in the life of the apostle Barnabas, as recorded in Acts 11:19-26 and 13:1-3. Barnabas was a disciple of Jesus Christ who was known for his encouragement and support of other believers.

In Acts 11:19-26, we see that Barnabas was sent by the church in Jerusalem to Antioch to encourage and support the believers there. When he arrived, he saw the grace of God and was glad, and he encouraged them all to remain faithful to the Lord.

In Acts 13:1-3, we see that Barnabas was part of a team of prophets and teachers in the church at Antioch, which included Saul (who would later become the apostle Paul). The Holy Spirit said to them, *"Set apart for me Barnabas and Saul for the work to which I have called them."* Then, after fasting and praying, they laid their hands on them and sent them off.

Barnabas' example shows us the importance of seeking accountability and support from other believers. He was part of a community of believers who encouraged, supported, and challenged him to live a life of sacrificial living.

Practice Spiritual Disciplines

We must practice spiritual disciplines such as prayer, fasting, and meditation, which can help us to cultivate a deeper and more intimate relationship with God. The best example we can find in the scriptures of practicing spiritual disciplines can be seen in the life of Jesus Christ, as recorded in Luke 4:1-2 and Matthew 4:1-2. Before beginning His public ministry, Jesus spent 40 days in the wilderness, fasting and praying.

In Luke 4:1-2, it is recorded that "*Jesus, full of the Holy Spirit, returned from the Jordan and was led around by the Spirit in the wilderness for forty days, being tempted by the devil. And He ate nothing during those days, and when they had ended, He became hungry.*"

Jesus' example shows us the importance of practicing spiritual disciplines such as prayer, fasting, and meditation. By spending time in prayer and fasting, Jesus was able to cultivate a deeper and more intimate relationship with God and to prepare Himself for the challenges and temptations that lay ahead.

Be Willing to Take Risks

We must be willing to take risks and step out in faith, trusting in God's sovereignty and provision. Being willing to take risks can be seen in the life of Abraham, as recorded in Genesis 12:1-9. God called Abraham to leave his home and family in Ur of the Chaldeans and to travel to a land that He would show him.

In Genesis 12:1, God says to Abraham, "*Go forth from your country, and from your relatives and from your father's house, to the land which I will show you.*" Abraham's response is recorded in Genesis 12:4, "*So Abram went forth as the Lord had spoken to him, and Lot went with him. Now Abram was seventy-five years old when he departed from Haran.*"

Abraham's willingness to take risks and step out in faith is evident in his decision to leave his home and family and travel to a land that he had never seen. He trusted in God's sovereignty and provision, knowing that He would provide and fulfill His promises.

Seek to Live a Life of Obedience

We must seek to live a life of obedience to God's Word, seeking to do His will and live according to His plans. An example of seeking to live a life of obedience can be seen in the life of Daniel, as recorded in Daniel 1:1-21 and 6:1-28. Daniel was a young Jewish man who was taken captive by the Babylonians and brought to the palace to serve King Nebuchadnezzar.

In Daniel 1:8, Daniel makes a decision to obey God's Word and to refuse to eat the king's food, which would have defiled him. Instead, he and his friends, Shadrach, Meshach, and Abednego, asked to be given vegetables and water to eat.

Daniel's obedience to God's Word is also seen in Daniel 6:1-28, where he refuses to stop praying to God, even when it becomes illegal to do so. Daniel's enemies, who were jealous of his position and influence, tricked the king into issuing a decree that no one could pray to anyone except the king for 30 days.

However, Daniel refused to obey the king's decree and continued to pray to God, even when it meant risking his life. In Daniel 6:10, it is recorded that *"he went home and got down on his knees three times a day, just as he had done before, and prayed and gave thanks before his God."*

Seek to Live a Life of Surrender

We must seek to live a life of surrender to God, seeking to let go of our own plans and desires and seek to live a life that is pleasing to Him. Seeking to live a life of surrender can be seen in the life of Jesus Christ, as recorded in John 4:34 and 5:30. Jesus said, *"My food is to do the will of Him who sent Me and to accomplish His work"* (John 4:34).

Jesus' life was a perfect example of surrender to God. He came to earth to do the will of His Father, and He lived His life in complete surrender to God's plans and purposes. In John 5:30, Jesus said, *"I can do nothing on My own initiative. As I hear, I judge; and My judgment is just, because I do not seek My own will, but the will of Him who sent Me."*

By following these steps, we can overcome The Sin of Ignoring, Neglecting, or Avoiding the Call to Sacrificial Living, and seek to live a life that is pleasing to God. May we be willing to surrender our lives, desires, and ambitions to God, and seek to

live a life of sacrificial living, advancing God's kingdom and glorifying Him in all that we do.

Final Thoughts

As we conclude this chapter, remember that the call to sacrificial living is a call to all believers. It is not optional, but rather it is a necessary part of our walk with God.

It is also important to remember that the rewards of sacrificial living are numerous and eternal. Let us remember that by living a life of sacrifice and service, we can experience a deeper and more intimate relationship with God, and we can experience the joy and satisfaction of seeing lives changed and transformed through our service and ministry.

Finally, remember that the consequences of ignoring the call to sacrificial living are severe and eternal. So, when we ignore, neglect, or avoid the call to sacrificial living, we can expect to experience a range of negative consequences, including the judgment and discipline of God.

I therefore encourage you to heed the call to sacrificial living and seek to live a life that is pleasing to God. Surrender your life, your desires, and your ambitions to God, and seek to live a life that is characterized by sacrifice, service, and surrender. God bless you.

Before you move to the next chapter, just pause for a while to pray this simple prayer:

"Father in the name of Jesus, by your power and authority, by your grace and mercy, I embrace the call to live sacrificially. I declare that because of my sacrificial living, my life will reveal the story of your glory. I am going for the best and the highest, and I separate myself from the sin of ignoring or avoiding living sacrificially in my living and my approach, I receive grace to reveal your glory in the name of Jesus."

CHAPTER SEVEN

The Sin of Ignoring, Disrespecting, and Avoiding Divine Processes in Pursuit of God's Purpose and Plans for Your Life.

"Let me make this clear: If someone doesn't walk through the door of the sheepfold, but climbs in some other way, that person is a thief and a robber. But the one who enters through the door is the shepherd of the sheep. The gatekeeper opens the gate for him, and the sheep hear his voice and come to him. He calls his own sheep by name and leads them out. When he gets them all out, he leads them and they follow because they know his voice. They won't follow a stranger; they'll run from him because they don't know his voice." - John 10:1-5 (MSG)

In the context of avoiding divine processes, John 10:1-5 (MSG) teaches us that there is only one way to enter into a deep and intimate relationship with God, and that is through the "door" of surrender, trust, and faith.

Jesus is the door, and He is the only way to enter into a relationship with God (John 14:6). When we try to climb in some other way, by bypassing the divine process and trying to achieve our goals and fulfill our divine purpose through our efforts and strength, we are like the thief and the robber who tried to climb into the sheepfold.

However, when we enter through the door of surrender, trust, and faith, we become like the shepherd of the sheep, who is led by the gatekeeper (the Holy Spirit) and who hears the voice of the shepherd (Jesus) and follows Him.

The divine process is like the sheepfold, where we are led by the shepherd (Jesus) and guided by the gatekeeper (the Holy Spirit). When we follow the divine process, we are led to a place of spiritual maturity and fulfillment, where we can fulfill our divine purpose and achieve our goals.

Divine process refers to the spiritual journey or path that an individual embarks upon to connect with God Almighty, achieve spiritual growth, and fulfill their divine purpose in life. It is a journey that requires patience, perseverance, and trust in God's sovereignty and provision.

Many Christians today are looking for shortcuts to achieve their goals and fulfill their divine purpose. They want to become what God wants them to become overnight. So, they want to climb the ladder of success without going through the necessary steps. They want to reap the benefits of spiritual growth without putting in the effort required to cultivate a deep and intimate relationship with God.

However, this approach is not only unscriptural but also unwise. It is like giving a 5 or 10-year-old child the keys to a Ferrari and expecting them to drive it safely without any training or experience. The result would be disastrous, and the child would likely end up in a crash. Let me share a story to explain this.

It was a sunny Saturday afternoon when five children, all in their early teens, decided to take a joyride in a turbo-engine car. The car, which belonged to one of their parents, was known for its speed and power. The children, who were all excited and eager to feel the rush of adrenaline, decided to take the car out for a spin without the permission of their parents.

As they drove down the highway, the driver, who was inexperienced and reckless, became carried away by the speed and power of the engine. He accelerated without control, thinking that he was invincible and that nothing could happen to him. The other children in the car were screaming with excitement and fear, but the driver was too caught up in the moment to listen to their warnings.

As they approached a sharp curve on the highway, the driver lost control of the car. The car skidded off the road and crashed into a tree, causing a massive explosion. All five children were killed instantly, their young lives cut short by the reckless and irresponsible behavior of the driver.

This tragic story has a powerful parallel with the way many people, including believers, seek to ignore the process and get ahead in life. Just like the driver of the turbo engine car, many people become carried away by the speed and power of shortcuts and quick fixes. They think that they can bypass the process and achieve their goals without putting in the necessary effort and time.

Just like the driver of the turbo-engine car, many people who ignore the process and seek to take shortcuts end up crashing and burning. They may experience temporary success or gains, but ultimately, they will not fulfill God's expectations for their lives.

The story of the five children and the turbo engine car serves as something we can all learn from the importance of embracing divine processes. God has a plan and purpose for each of our lives, and He has ordained a process by which we can achieve our goals, fulfill our divine purpose, and become the best and the highest.

Let's also look into the story of **King Saul**, who avoided the divine process and ultimately crashed and burned. Saul was chosen by God to be the first king of Israel, but he struggled with impatience and a lack of trust in God's timing.

> "He waited seven days, the time set by Samuel; but Samuel did not come to Gilgal, and Saul's men began to scatter. So he said, "Bring me the burnt offering and the fellowship offerings." And Saul offered up the burnt offering. Just as he finished making the

offering, Samuel arrived, and Saul went out to greet him. What
have you done?" asked Samuel. Saul replied, "When I saw that
the men were scattering and that you did not come at the set
time, and that the Philistines were assembling at Michmash,
I thought, 'Now the Philistines will come down against me
at Gilgal, and I have not sought the Lord's favor.' So I felt
compelled to offer the burnt offering. You have done a foolish
thing," Samuel said. "You have not kept the command the Lord
your God gave you; if you had, he would have established your
kingdom over Israel for all time. But now your kingdom will not
endure; the Lord has sought out a man after his own heart and
appointed him ruler of his people because you
have not kept the Lord's command."
1 Samuel 13:8-14 (NIV)

When Samuel, the prophet, didn't arrive on time to offer sacrifices, Saul took matters into his own hands and offered the sacrifices himself. This was a direct violation of God's instructions, and it led to severe consequences. God rejected Saul as king, and his reign was marked by failure and tragedy.

Saul's story teaches us that **impulsiveness and a lack of patience can lead to devastating consequences**. When we try to rush ahead of God's plan, we can end up missing out on His best for our lives. Instead, we should learn to trust in God's timing and wait for His guidance.

When we ignore the process and seek to take shortcuts, we are essentially trying to bypass God's plan and purpose for our lives. We are trying to achieve our goals through our strength and effort, rather than trusting in God's sovereignty and provision.

However, when we embrace divine processes, we are essentially trusting in God's sovereignty and provision. We recognize that God has a plan and purpose for our lives and that He will guide and direct us as we seek to achieve our goals and fulfill our divine purpose.

Similarly, when we try to bypass the divine process and take shortcuts to achieve our goals, we are likely to end up in a spiritual crash. We may experience temporary success or achievements, but they will not be sustainable, and we will ultimately end up in a place of spiritual dryness and stagnation.

The truth is that there is a process to every progress in the kingdom of God. We cannot bypass the process and expect to achieve lasting results. We must be willing to go through the process, to trust in God's sovereignty and provision, and to wait on His timing.

The divine process involves surrender, trust, and faith. It involves letting go of our plans and desires and seeking to align ourselves with God's plans and purposes. It involves trusting in God's sovereignty, even when we do not understand what He is doing. It involves having faith that God will fulfill His promises and bring us to a place of spiritual maturity and fulfillment, making us the best and the highest.

As we journey through the divine process, we will encounter various challenges and obstacles. We will face times of testing and trial, where our faith and trust in God will be stretched to the limit. We will face times of uncertainty and doubt, where we will question God's plans and purposes. And we will face times of fear and anxiety, where we will be tempted to give up and abandon the journey.

However, it is in these moments of challenge and uncertainty that we must draw on the resources of God's grace and mercy. We must trust in His sovereignty and provision, knowing that He is working everything out for our good. We must have faith that He will bring us through the difficult times and into a place of spiritual maturity and fulfillment.

The Sin of Ignoring, Disrespecting, and Avoiding Divine Processes

The sin of ignoring, disrespecting, and avoiding divine processes refers to the act of disregarding or bypassing the spiritual journey or path that God has ordained for an individual's life. It involves neglecting or rejecting the processes, principles, and patterns that God has established for spiritual growth, development, and fulfillment. It is going through the window instead of the gate, which is exactly what a thief and a robber would do. This sin can manifest in various ways, and we must identify them, avoid them, and overcome them.

Impatience and Haste

Rushing through or bypassing the divine process in an attempt to achieve quick results or instant gratification. Impatience and haste are two of the most significant obstacles to fulfilling God's purpose and plans for our lives. When we rush through or bypass the divine process, we can end up missing out on the spiritual growth, development, and transformation that God intends for us. If you start from zero to a hundred miles per minute, it will kill you because that's a high speed. It is being in
unnecessary haste.

Abraham and Sarah's decision to have a child through Hagar, Sarah's servant, is an example of impatience and haste. They rushed through the divine process and tried to take matters into their own hands, which led to conflict and tension (Genesis 16:1- 16).

Moses' decision to strike the rock twice, rather than speaking to it as God had instructed, is an example of impatience and haste. Moses' actions were motivated by a desire to get quick results and to appease the people, rather than trusting in God's sovereignty and timing (Numbers 20:2-12).

Disobedience and Rebellion

Refusing to follow God's instructions, guidance, or principles, and instead, following one's desires, plans, or agendas. Disobedience and rebellion are also significant
obstacles to fulfilling God's purpose and plans for our lives. When we refuse to follow God's instructions, guidance, or principles, and instead follow our desires, plans, or agendas, we are essentially rebelling against God's authority and sovereignty.

Adam and Eve's decision to eat the forbidden fruit is an example of disobedience and rebellion. They refused to follow God's instructions and instead followed their desires and plans (Genesis 3:1-7).

The Israelites' refusal to enter the Promised Land due to fear and unbelief is an example of disobedience and rebellion. They refused to follow God's instructions and instead followed their desires and plans (Numbers 13-14).

Lack of Trust and Faith

Failing to trust in God's sovereignty, wisdom, and timing, and instead, relying on one's strength, abilities, or resources. A lack of trust and faith is a significant obstacle to fulfilling God's purpose and plans for our lives. When we fail to trust in God's sovereignty, wisdom, and timing, and instead rely on our strength, abilities, or
resources, we are essentially saying that we don't need God or His guidance.

Peter's lack of trust and faith in Jesus' plan and purpose led to his denial of Jesus (Matthew 26:69-75).

The rich young ruler's lack of trust and faith in Jesus' teaching and guidance led to his inability to follow Jesus (Matthew 19:16-22).

Pride and Self-sufficiency

Believing that one can achieve their goals or fulfill their purpose without God's help, guidance, or empowerment. Pride and self-sufficiency are two of the most significant obstacles to fulfilling God's purpose and plans for our lives. When we believe that we can achieve our goals or fulfill our purpose without God's help, guidance, or
empowerment, we are essentially saying that we don't need God or His involvement in our lives.

The story of the Tower of Babel is an example of pride and

self-sufficiency. The people of Babel tried to build a tower that would reach the heavens, without God's help or guidance (Genesis 11:1-9).

King Nebuchadnezzar's pride and self-sufficiency led to his downfall. He believed that he was the one who had built Babylon and achieved its greatness, without acknowledging God's sovereignty and involvement (Daniel 4:28-37).

The Pharisees' pride and self-sufficiency led to their spiritual blindness and hardness of heart. They believed that they could achieve righteousness and salvation through their efforts and obedience to the law, without recognizing their need for God's grace and mercy (Matthew 23:1-36).

The Right Way to Fulfill Your Divine Purpose in Life

Fulfilling your divine purpose in life requires following divine processes, principles, and instructions. It's essential to understand that there is a process to every progress in the kingdom of God. In the remaining part of this chapter, we'll be looking at the right ways to fulfill your divine purpose in life, as outlined in the Bible.

Salvation

The first step in fulfilling your divine purpose is to gain salvation through faith in Jesus Christ. Salvation is the foundation of our relationship with God and is essential for spiritual growth and development. Jesus said, *"For God so loved the world that he gave his one and only Son, that whoever believes in him shall not perish but have eternal life"* (John 3:16). The Bible also says, *"If you confess with your mouth that Jesus is Lord and believe in your heart that God raised him from the dead, you will be saved"* (Romans 10:9-10).

Sanctification

Sanctification is the process of being set apart for God's purpose. It involves separating ourselves from sin and worldly influences and dedicating ourselves to God's will and purposes. The Bible says, *"It is God's will that you should be sanctified: that you should avoid sexual immorality; that each of you should learn to control your own body in a way that is holy and honorable"* (1 Thessalonians 4:3-4). It also says, *"Make every effort to live in peace with everyone and to be holy; without holiness, no one will see the Lord"* (Hebrews 12:14).

Consecration

Consecration involves dedicating ourselves to God's service and surrendering our lives to His will and purposes. It's a commitment to live a life that is pleasing to God. The Bible says, *"Therefore, I urge you, brothers and sisters, in view of God's mercy, to offer your bodies as a living sacrifice, holy and pleasing to God—this is your true and proper worship"* (Romans 12:1-2). It also says, *"If anyone cleanses himself from what is dishonorable, he will be a vessel for honorable use, set apart as holy, useful to the master of the house, ready for every good work"* (2 Timothy 2:21).

Holy Spirit Baptism

The Holy Spirit baptism is a supernatural experience that empowers us to live a life that is pleasing to God. It's essential for spiritual growth, development, and empowerment. The Bible says, *"Repent and be baptized, every one of you, in the name of Jesus Christ for the forgiveness of your sins. And you will receive the gift of the Holy Spirit"* (Acts 2:38). It also says, *"For we were all baptized by one Spirit so as to form one body—whether Jews or Gentiles, slave or free—and we were all given the one Spirit to drink"* (1 Corinthians 12:13).

Becoming a Disciple

Becoming a disciple involves committing ourselves to follow Jesus Christ and learn from Him. It's a lifelong process of growth, development, and transformation. The Bible says, *"Therefore go and make disciples of all nations, baptizing them in the name of the Father and of the Son and of the Holy Spirit, and teaching them to obey everything I have commanded you"* (Matthew 28:19-20). It also says, *"Then he called the crowd to him along with his disciples and said: 'Whoever wants to be my disciple must deny themselves and take up their cross daily and follow me"'* (Luke 9:23-25).

Becoming a Laborer in the Kingdom of Christ

Becoming a laborer in the kingdom of Christ involves using our gifts, talents, and abilities to serve God and advance His kingdom. It's a call to be fruitful and productive in our service to God. The Bible says, *"Then he said to his disciples, 'The harvest is plentiful but the workers are few. Ask the Lord of the harvest, therefore, to send out workers into his harvest field"'* (Matthew 9:37-38). It also says, *"He told them,*
'The harvest is plentiful, but the workers are few. Ask the Lord of the harvest, therefore, to send out workers into his harvest field"' (Luke 10:2).

Embracing God's Purpose for Your Life

Embracing God's purpose for your life involves understanding and accepting God's plan and purpose for your life. It's essential to trust in God's sovereignty and timing. The Bible says, *"For I know the plans I have for you,"* declares the Lord, *"plans to prosper you and not to harm you, plans to give you hope and a future"* (Jeremiah 29:11). It also says, *"And we know that in all things God works for the good of those who love him, who have been called according to his purpose"* (Romans 8:28).

Submission

Submission involves humbling ourselves and submitting to God's will and purposes. It's essential to recognize God's authority and sovereignty in our lives. The Bible says, *"Submit yourselves, then, to God. Resist the devil, and he will flee from you"* (James 4:7). It also says, *"Humble yourselves, therefore, under God's mighty hand, that he may lift you up in due time"* (1 Peter 5:6).

Humility

Humility involves recognizing our limitations and weaknesses, and depending on God's strength and empowerment. It's essential to cultivate a humble heart and attitude. The Bible says, *"Humility and the fear of the Lord bring wealth and honor and life"* (Proverbs 22:4). It also says, *"All of you, clothe yourselves with humility toward one another, because, 'God opposes the proud but shows favor to the humble'"* (1 Peter 5:5-6).

Loyalty

Loyalty involves being faithful and committed to God and His kingdom. It's essential to cultivate a loyal heart and attitude and to be willing to stand firm in our commitment to God. The Bible says, *"Who then is the faithful and wise servant, whom the master has put in charge of the servants in his household to give them their food at the proper time? It will be good for that servant whose master finds him doing so when he returns"* (Matthew 24:45-47). It also says, *"Be faithful, even to the point of death, and I will give you life as your victor's crown"* (Revelation 2:10).

Fulfilling your divine purpose in life requires following divine processes, principles, and instructions. It's essential to understand that there is a process to every progress in the kingdom of God. By following the right ways outlined in this chapter, you can fulfill your divine purpose in life and live a life that is pleasing to God.

Overcoming the Sin of Ignoring, Disrespecting, and Avoiding Divine Processes

Ignoring, disrespecting, and avoiding divine processes in pursuit of God's purpose and plans for your life is a serious sin that can hinder your spiritual growth and development. To overcome this sin, you must first recognize and acknowledge your actions, and then take steps to correct them.

Recognize and Acknowledge Your Actions

The first step in overcoming the sin of ignoring, disrespecting, and avoiding divine processes is to recognize and acknowledge your actions. You must take responsibility for your decisions and actions, and acknowledge the harm

that they have caused.
The Bible says, "*If we claim to be without sin, we deceive ourselves and the truth is not in us*" (1 John 1:8).

Repent and Confess Your Sin

Once you have recognized and acknowledged your actions, you must repent and confess your sins. Repentance involves turning away from your sin and turning towards God, while confession involves acknowledging your sin and seeking forgiveness. The Bible says, "*If we confess our sins, he is faithful and just and will forgive us our sins and purify us from all unrighteousness*" (1 John 1:9).

Seek God's Forgiveness and Mercy

After repenting and confessing your sin, you must seek God's forgiveness and mercy. God is a loving and merciful God who desires to forgive and restore us. The Bible says, "*The Lord is compassionate and gracious, slow to anger, abounding in love*" (Psalm 103:8).

Commit Yourself to Follow Divine Processes

To overcome the sin of ignoring, disrespecting, and avoiding divine processes, you must commit yourself to following divine processes. This involves seeking God's guidance and direction and trusting in His sovereignty, wisdom, and timing. The Bible says, "*Trust in the Lord with all your heart and lean not on your understanding; in all your ways submit to him, and he will make your paths straight*" (Proverbs 3:5-6).

Surround Yourself with Supportive People

Surrounding yourself with supportive people who will encourage and support you as you seek to follow divine processes is essential. The Bible says, "*As iron sharpens iron, so one person sharpens another*" (Proverbs 27:17).

Stay Focused and Committed

Finally, staying focused and committed to following divine processes is crucial. The Bible says, "*Let us fix our eyes on Jesus, the author and perfecter of our faith, who for the joy set before him endured the cross, scorning its shame, and sat down at the right hand of the throne of God*" (Hebrews 12:2).

Ignoring, disrespecting, and avoiding divine processes in pursuit of God's purpose and plans for your life is a serious sin that can hinder your spiritual growth, and development and hinder you from becoming the best and the highest. However, by recognizing and acknowledging your actions, repenting and confessing your sin, seeking God's forgiveness and mercy, committing yourself to follow divine processes, surrounding yourself with supportive people, and staying focused and committed, you can overcome this sin and fulfill your divine purpose in life.

Before you move to the next chapter where we will be discussing the fifth sin, just pause for a while to pray this simple prayer:

"Father in the name of Jesus, by Your power and authority, by Your grace and mercy I give you praise for Your grace and kindness, I thank You for being a faithful God to me and my household. Lord, I pray that You enable me to be the very best in your kingdom and to be used for Your highest purposes. I declare my life is Yours, use me for miracles, signs, and wonders to heal the sick, raise the dead, save my generation, turn lives around, use me to bring financial glory, to change my generation and my world for your highest purposes in the name of Jesus."

CHAPTER EIGHT

The Sin of Failing to Come to Jesus to Give You an Experience, Freedom, and Satisfaction.

"Let me make this clear: If someone doesn't enter the sheep pen through the gate, climbing in some other way, who is he? He's a thief or a wolf. For a shepherd enters through the gate. The gatekeeper opens the gate for him, and the sheep recognize his voice and come to him. He calls his own sheep by name and leads them out. When he gets them all out, he leads them and they follow because they are familiar with his voice. They won't follow a stranger; they'll run from him because they don't know his voice." - John 10:1-9 (MSG)

In the context of failing to come to Jesus to give you an experience, freedom, and satisfaction, this passage throws light on the importance of coming to Jesus through the right gate. Jesus is the gate, and He is the only way to experience true freedom and satisfaction.

In this passage, the gatekeeper represents God the Father. The gatekeeper opens the gate for the shepherd, Jesus, to enter and lead the sheep out. This represents God's sovereignty and control over our lives. God has given Jesus the authority to lead us and provide for our needs.

The sheep in this passage represent believers who have put their faith in Jesus. The sheep recognize the shepherd's voice and come to Him because they are familiar with

His voice. This represents the intimate relationship that we can have with Jesus. When we come to Jesus, we can experience a deep sense of peace, joy, and satisfaction.

The passage also warns us about the dangers of following strangers or false shepherds. When we try to find experience, freedom, and satisfaction outside of Jesus, we can end up following strangers or false shepherds who promise us the world but deliver nothing but emptiness and despair.

The Sin of Not Coming to Jesus or Trusting Jesus to Care for You

The sin of not coming to Jesus or trusting Jesus to care for you is a fundamental error that can lead to a life of frustration, disappointment, and unfulfillment. Jesus cares about every detail of our lives, and He desires to provide for our needs, protect us from harm, and give us a sense of purpose and direction.

However, many people fail to trust Jesus to care for them. Instead, they rely on their strength, resources, and abilities to navigate life's challenges. This is a sin because it demonstrates a lack of faith and trust in Jesus' ability to care for us.

The Sin of Not Coming to Jesus to Ask for Care When You Need Care

Another aspect of this sin is failing to come to Jesus to ask for care when we need it. Jesus is always available to provide for our needs, but we must come to Him and ask. The Bible says, *"Ask and it will be given to you; seek and you will find; knock and the door will be opened to you"* (Matthew 7:7).

However, many people fail to ask Jesus for care when they need it. Instead, they try to handle their problems on their own, or they seek help from other sources. This is a sin because it demonstrates a lack of dependence on Jesus and a lack of trust in His ability to provide for our needs.

Jesus cares about every detail of our lives. He cares about our physical, emotional, and spiritual needs. He cares about our relationships, our careers, and our finances. He cares about our struggles, our challenges, and our difficulties.

The Bible says, *"Cast all your anxiety on him because he cares for you"* (1 Peter 5:7). Jesus wants us to come to Him with our needs, our concerns, and our worries. He wants to provide for us, protect us, and give us a sense of purpose and direction.

Failing to come to Jesus for experience, freedom, and satisfaction can have serious consequences in our lives. It can lead to a life of frustration, disappointment, and unfulfillment. It can cause us to feel anxious, worried, and fearful. It can lead to spiritual stagnation and decline.

On the other hand, coming to Jesus for experience, freedom, and satisfaction can bring numerous benefits. It can give us a sense of purpose and direction. It can provide for our physical, emotional, and spiritual needs. It can protect us from harm and give us a sense of security and safety.

Jesus Will Give You Satisfaction

Jesus wants to give us life satisfaction. He wants to provide for our needs, protect us from harm, and give us a sense of purpose and direction. The Bible says, *"Delight yourself in the Lord, and he will give you the desires of your heart"* (Psalm 37:4).

Jesus will give us satisfaction using many different things. He may use our relationships, our careers, our finances, or our hobbies to bring us satisfaction. He may use our struggles, our challenges, and our difficulties to teach us valuable lessons and bring us closer to Himself.

Jesus Wants to Set You Free

Jesus wants to set us free from the things that bind us. He wants to free us from sin, from fear, from anxiety, and from worry. He wants to give us freedom to live life to the fullest, to pursue our passions, and to fulfill our purpose.

The Bible says, *"So if the Son sets you free, you will be free indeed"* (John 8:36). Jesus is the only one who can truly set us free. He is the only one who can forgive our sins, heal our emotional wounds, and give us a sense of purpose and direction.

Never Allow Yourself to Be Jealous of Others

Never allow yourself to be jealous of others. Jealousy is a sin that can consume our hearts and minds, causing us to focus on what others have rather than what God has given us. The Bible says, "*So don't be jealous of others or begin to wish you were them. For their lives are not worth imitating*" (Proverbs 3:31, MSG).

Instead of being jealous of others, we should focus on our relationship with God and seek to fulfill our purpose and plans. We should trust in God's sovereignty and timing, knowing that He has a unique plan for each of our lives.

The story of the rich young ruler is a very good example of someone who failed to come to Jesus to get experience, freedom, and satisfaction. The story begins with a rich young ruler approaching Jesus and asking, "*Teacher, what good thing must I do to get eternal life?*" (Matthew 19:16). Jesus responds by telling him to keep the commandments, and the young ruler claims to have done so since he was a child.

However, Jesus looks at him with love and says, "*If you want to be perfect, go, sell your possessions and give to the poor, and you will have treasure in heaven. Then come, follow me*" (Matthew 19:21). The young ruler is shocked and saddened by Jesus' words, and he walks away because he has great wealth.

This is a clear illustration of the failure of the rich young ruler to come to Jesus to get experience, freedom, and satisfaction. Despite his wealth and outward appearance of righteousness, the young ruler was lacking in true spiritual life and satisfaction.

He failed to recognize that Jesus was offering him something far greater than his wealth and possessions. Jesus was offering him eternal life, a treasure in heaven, and a deeper experience of God's love and presence that will make him become the best and highest.

The story of the rich young ruler points out several lessons that we can learn from and avoid falling into the sin of *Failing to Come to Jesus to Give You Experience, Freedom, and Satisfaction.*

Wealth and possessions are not the source of true satisfaction: The rich young ruler had great wealth, but he was still lacking in true spiritual life and satisfaction. Wealth and possessions are often touted as the key to happiness and satisfaction. Many people believe that if they can just accumulate enough wealth and possessions, they will finally be content and fulfilled. However, this is a deception.

The Limits of Wealth and Possessions

Wealth and possessions can provide a temporary sense of satisfaction and pleasure, but they are limited in their ability to provide true and lasting fulfillment. They can also become a source of stress, anxiety, and worry, as we constantly strive to accumulate more and protect what we already have.

Furthermore, wealth and possessions can also create a sense of separation and isolation from others. When we focus too much on accumulating wealth and possessions, we can begin to see others as mere objects or obstacles to our success, rather than as fellow human beings or fellow believers worthy of our love, respect, and compassion.

The True Source of Satisfaction

So, what is the true source of satisfaction? The Bible tells us that true satisfaction and fulfillment come from knowing and following God. In Psalm 16:11, David writes, *"You make known to me the path of life; you will fill me with joy in your presence, with eternal pleasures at your right hand."*

Jesus also teaches us that true satisfaction and fulfillment come from seeking first the kingdom of God and His righteousness. In Matthew 6:33, He says, *"But seek first his kingdom and his righteousness, and all these things will be given to you as well."*

Jesus offers us something far greater than our wealth and possessions: Jesus offered the rich young ruler eternal life, a treasure in heaven, and a deeper experience of God's love and presence. Jesus offers us something far greater than our wealth and possessions. While wealth and possessions may provide temporary comfort and security, they are limited in their ability to provide true and lasting fulfillment.

In contrast, Jesus offers us eternal life, treasure in heaven, and a deeper experience of God's love and presence. These are gifts that transcend the fleeting nature of wealth and possessions and provide a sense of purpose, meaning, and fulfillment that cannot be found in material things.

Eternal Life

The gift of eternal life is perhaps the most significant offer of Jesus. Eternal life is not just a future hope, but a present reality that can be experienced through a personal relationship with Jesus. It is a life that is characterized by joy, peace, and purpose and is not limited by the constraints of time and space.

Treasure in Heaven

In addition to eternal life, Jesus also offers us treasure in heaven. This treasure is not just a future reward, but a present reality that can be experienced through our
relationship with Jesus. It is a treasure that is characterized by its eternal value and is not subject to the fluctuations of the market or the ravages of time.

A Deeper Experience of God's Love and Presence

Finally, Jesus offers us a deeper experience of God's love and presence. This experience is not just a feeling or an emotion, but a profound sense of connection and intimacy with God. It is an experience that is characterized by joy, peace, and contentment and is not limited by our circumstances or situation.

When Jesus offered the rich young ruler eternal life, treasure in heaven, and a deeper experience of God's love and presence, he responded with sadness and disappointment. He was unwilling to give up his wealth and possessions, and as a result, he missed out on the opportunity to experience the superior offer of Jesus.

We must be willing to let go of our attachments to the world: The rich young ruler was unwilling to let go of his wealth and possessions, and as a result, he missed out on the opportunity to experience true spiritual life and satisfaction. We must be willing to let go of our attachments to the world. This is a crucial step in experiencing true spiritual life and satisfaction. The rich young ruler's story illustrates the importance of letting go of our attachments to the world.

The rich young ruler was unwilling to let go of his wealth and possessions, and as a result, he missed out on the opportunity to experience true spiritual life and satisfaction which is a true picture of becoming the best and highest. His attachment to his wealth and possessions prevented him from following Jesus and experiencing the freedom and fulfillment that comes from knowing and following Him.

Letting go of our attachments to the world requires surrender and trust. We must surrender our attachments to God and trust that He has something better in store for us – becoming the best and the highest.

This is not always easy. It requires faith and obedience. But the rewards are well worth it. When we let go of our attachments to the world, we can experience a deeper sense of freedom and fulfillment. We can experience the joy and peace that comes from knowing and following God.

Jesus calls us to follow Him: Jesus called the rich young ruler to follow Him, but the young ruler was unwilling to do so. Jesus calls us to follow Him. This is a central theme of the Bible and a fundamental aspect of the Christian faith. Jesus calls us to follow Him, not just to believe in Him or acknowledge Him as Lord, but to follow Him in our daily lives.

The Cost of Following Jesus

Following Jesus requires sacrifice and obedience. It requires us to put God's will above our desires and interests. It requires us to be willing to give up things that are important to us, such as our wealth, our status, and our comfort.

Jesus taught that following Him would require sacrifice and obedience. He said, "*If anyone would come after me, let him deny himself and take up his cross and follow me*" (Matthew 16:24). He also said, "*Whoever wants to save their life will lose it, but whoever loses their life for me will find it*" (Matthew 16:25).

The Benefits of Following Jesus

Despite the cost, following Jesus is the most rewarding and fulfilling decision we can make. When we follow Jesus, we experience a deep sense of purpose and meaning. We experience a sense of joy and peace that transcends our circumstances. We experience a sense of freedom and liberation from the things that once held us back.

Following Jesus also gives us a sense of belonging and identity. We become part of a community of believers who are committed to following Jesus and living according to His teachings. We experience a sense of unity and solidarity with other believers, and we are able to support and encourage one another as we follow Jesus.

As we continue on our journey to understanding the sin of failing to come to Jesus, we must acknowledge the importance of recognizing our need for care and provision. Let's continue to explore the significance of acknowledging our need to be cared for and how this recognition can lead us to experience the freedom and satisfaction that only Jesus can provide.

Acknowledging Your Need to Be Cared For

The first step in overcoming the sin of failing to come to Jesus is to acknowledge our need to be cared for. This means recognizing that we are not self-sufficient, but rather, we need God's care and provision in our lives.

As the Bible says, "*Acknowledge and take to heart this day that the Lord is God in heaven above and on the earth below. There is no other*" (Deuteronomy 4:39). We must acknowledge God's sovereignty and power, and recognize our need for His care and provision.

Acknowledging That the Highest Care Comes from God

Not only must we acknowledge our need to be cared for, but we must also acknowledge that the highest care comes from God. We must recognize that God is our loving Father who desires to provide for our needs, protect us from harm, and give us a sense of purpose and direction.

As the Bible says, "*Which of you, if your son asks for bread, will give him a stone? Or if he asks for a fish, will give him a snake? If you, then, though you are evil, know how to give good gifts to your children, how much more will your Father in heaven give good gifts to those who ask him!*" (Matthew 7:9-11).

Itemizing Your Care

Once we have acknowledged our need to be cared for and recognized that the highest care comes from God, we must itemize our care. This means identifying the specific areas of our lives where we need God's care and provision.

As the Bible says, "*Commit to the Lord whatever you do, and he will establish your plans*" (Proverbs 16:3). We must commit our ways to God and trust in His care and provision.

Highlighting the Areas of Life, You Need to Be Cared For

As we itemize our care, we must highlight the areas of our lives where we need God's care and provision. This may include our health, wealth, family, ministry, or other areas of our lives.

As the Bible says, "*Cast all your anxiety on him because he cares for you*" (1 Peter 5:7). We must cast our cares and anxieties on God, trusting in His care and provision.

Presenting Your Care to God

Once we have itemized our care and highlighted the areas of our lives where we need God's care and provision, we must present our care to God. This means asking God to care for us and provide for our needs.

As the Bible says, *"This is the confidence we have in approaching God: that if we ask anything according to his will, he hears us"* (1 John 5:14). We must approach God with confidence, asking Him to care for us and provide for our needs.

Appreciating and Thanking God for His Care

Finally, we must appreciate and thank God for His care and provision in our lives. This means recognizing how God has cared for us and provided for our needs, and expressing our gratitude to Him.

As the Bible says, *"Give thanks to the Lord, for he is good; his love endures forever!"* (Psalm 107:1). We must give thanks to God for His care and provision, recognizing that His love endures forever.

Revealing God's Care to the World

We are living in days and times where revealing God's care and love to the world is crucial. If we want to show the world that God cares, we must allow Him to demonstrate His care and provision in our lives.

This requires trust and surrender. We must trust that God is good and that He desires to care for us. We must surrender our lives to Him, acknowledging that we are not self-sufficient, but rather, we need His care and provision.

A Prayer of Surrender

Take a little time to say this prayer that can help you surrender your life to God and ask for His care and provision:

"Lord, I want the best. I want the highest. I am sorry for not trusting you enough to care for me. Now, I am your baby, I am calling, I need care! Take care of me, Lord."

Overcoming the Sin of Failing to Come to Jesus

To overcome the sin of failing to come to Jesus and

experience the freedom and satisfaction that He provides, we must take several steps. First, we must purge ourselves by acknowledging that there are things in us that must go. This requires humility and a willingness to surrender to God's transformative power.

Taking Advantage of the Provisions in Christ

One of the most important steps in purging ourselves and overcoming the sin of failing to come to Jesus is to take advantage of the provisions in Christ. The blood of Jesus cleanses us from our sins, as stated in 1 John 1:6-7 MSG. When we accept Jesus as our Lord and Savior, His blood covers our sins, and we are made clean.

Engaging the Word

Another crucial step in purging ourselves and overcoming the sin of failing to come to Jesus is to engage in the word of God. The word of God is a spiritual laxative that purifies and cleanses us. As Psalm 119:9 TPT says, "How can a young person live a clean life? By carefully reading the Scriptures and living according to their teachings!" When we engage in the word of God, we are transformed by its power, and we become more like Jesus.

The word of God also gives us the power to defeat sin. As Ephesians 5:26 TPT says, "*Now you are clean and sanctified, and you have been made holy. You are presented to Him as a bride without any flaws!*" When we engage in the word of God, we are empowered to live a life that is pleasing to God, and we can defeat sin and its destructive power.

The Role of the Holy Spirit

The Holy Spirit also plays a vital role in purging ourselves and overcoming the sin of failing to come to Jesus. As Romans 8:13 TPT says, "*For when you live controlled by the flesh, you are about to die. But if the life of the Spirit puts to death the corrupt ways of the flesh, we then live.*" The Holy Spirit gives us the ability to defeat sin and live a victorious life.

Submitting to Spiritual Leadership and Mentorship

Submitting to spiritual leadership and mentorship is also essential in purging ourselves and overcoming the sin of failing to come to Jesus. However, it is crucial to submit to leaders who will guide and support you, rather than those who will use your failures to shame you.

The Importance of Humility

Humility is also a vital component in purging ourselves and overcoming the sin of failing to come to Jesus. As the Bible says, *"Humble yourselves, therefore, under God's mighty hand, that he may lift you up in due time"* (1 Peter 5:6). When we humble ourselves, we open ourselves up to God's transformative power and His ability to lift us up.

The Power of Fellowship

Embracing fellowship with other believers is also essential in purging ourselves and overcoming the sin of failing to come to Jesus. As the Bible says, *"Let us consider how we may spur one another on toward love and good deeds"* (Hebrews 10:24). When we fellowship with other believers, we are encouraged and supported in our walk with God.

The Power of Praise

Finally, giving yourself constantly to praise, worship, and thanksgiving is essential in purging yourself and overcoming the sin of failing to come to Jesus. As the Bible says, *"Is anyone among you in trouble? Let them pray. Is anyone happy? Let them sing songs of praise"* (James 5:13). Praise brings deliverance, and it is a powerful tool in overcoming sin and experiencing the freedom and satisfaction that Jesus provides.

Overcoming the sin of failing to come to Jesus and experiencing the freedom and satisfaction that He provides requires a deep understanding of God's transformative power and His desire to care for and provide for His children. It requires humility, surrender, and a willingness to engage with God's word and the Holy Spirit. By taking advantage of the provisions in Christ, engaging the word, submitting to spiritual leadership and mentorship, and embracing fellowship and praise, we can purge ourselves and overcome the sin of failing to come to Jesus.

As we conclude this chapter on the sin of failing to come to Jesus to give you an experience, freedom, and satisfaction, we are reminded of the importance of trusting in Jesus' ability to care for us. Jesus is the gate, and He is the only way to experience true freedom and satisfaction.

To become the best and the highest, we must come to Jesus and trust in His ability to care for us. We must recognize that Jesus cares about every detail of our lives, and
He desires to provide for our needs, protect us from harm, and give us a sense of purpose and direction.

We must also acknowledge that failing to come to Jesus for experience, freedom, and satisfaction can have serious consequences in our lives. It can lead to a life of frustration, disappointment, and unfulfillment. It can cause us to feel anxious, worried, and fearful. It can lead to spiritual stagnation and decline.

On the other hand, coming to Jesus for experience, freedom, and satisfaction can bring numerous benefits. It can give us a sense of purpose and direction. It can provide for our physical, emotional, and spiritual needs. It can protect us from harm and give us a sense of security and safety.

As we strive to become the best and the highest, let us remember that Jesus is the only one who can truly satisfy our deepest longings and desires. He is the only one who can set us free from the things that bind us. Let us come to Jesus with humility and trust, and let us experience the freedom and satisfaction that only He can provide.

In the words of Psalm 37:4, "*Delight yourself in the Lord, and he will give you the desires of your heart.*" Let us delight ourselves in the Lord, and let us trust in His ability to care for us and provide for our needs.

Remember that becoming the best and the highest requires a deep understanding of God's transformative power and His desire to care for and provide for His children. It requires humility, trust, and a willingness to come to Jesus and ask for care. Let us strive to become the best and the highest, and let us experience the freedom and satisfaction that only Jesus can provide.

CONCLUSION

Stand Out and Enjoy the Best and Highest Life

Joseph's story is found in Genesis, chapters 37-50. Joseph was a young man who had a big dream from God. He dreamt that he would one day stand out in life, be a great leader and his family would bow down to him.

However, Joseph's journey to fulfilling his dream was not easy. He faced many challenges and setbacks, including being betrayed by his brothers, sold into slavery, and falsely accused by his master's wife.

Despite these challenges, Joseph never gave up on his dream. He continued to trust in God's plan and purpose for his life and remained faithful and obedient to God's will.

Eventually, Joseph's dream was fulfilled, and he became a great leader in Egypt. He was second in command to Pharaoh, and he was able to use his position to bless his family and the entire nation of Israel.

What it Means to Stand Out and Enjoy the Best and Highest Life.

Joseph's story illustrates what it means to stand out and enjoy the best and highest life. It means trusting in God's plan and purpose for your life, even when the journey is difficult and uncertain.

It means remaining faithful and obedient to God's will, even when it's hard. It means persevering through challenges and setbacks and staying committed to your values and passions.

Ultimately, standing out and enjoying the best and highest life means fulfilling your God-given destiny and living a life that is true to who you are. It means using your unique talents and gifts to make a positive impact in the world and experiencing a sense of purpose, fulfillment, and joy that comes from living a life that is aligned with God's will and purpose.

As Joseph's story shows, enjoying the best and highest life is not always easy, but it is always worth it. When we trust in God's plan and purpose for our lives and remain faithful and obedient to His will, we can experience a life of purpose, fulfillment, and joy that is beyond our wildest dreams.

As I reflect on my journey, I am reminded of the power of following God's plan for my life. From the moment I encountered the Lord in 1995, I knew that I had a specific mandate to fulfill. God gave me a clear vision to wipe away tears from the faces of all mankind and to bring humanity into God's fullness for their lives.

As I surrendered to God's will and purpose, I began to experience a sense of purpose and direction that I had never known before. I relocated from Nigeria to Illinois in 2005 and established the headquarters of my ministry, Church on Fire International (COFI). Today, COFI has multiple locations across the globe, and I have the privilege of serving as the presiding Apostle.

Throughout my journey, I have learned that following God's plan for my life requires trust, obedience, and perseverance. There have been many challenges and setbacks along the way, but I have always tried to stay focused on God's vision and purpose for my life.

As a result of following God's plan, I have experienced a level of success and fulfillment that I never thought possible. I have been able to use my gifts and talents to make a positive impact in the world, and I have been blessed with a loving family and a thriving ministry.

But more than anything, I have learned that following God's plan for my life is not just about achieving success or fulfillment; it's about standing out and becoming the best and highest version of myself. It's about living a life that is true to who I am and using my unique gifts and talents to make a positive difference in the world.

Following God's plan for my life has been the key to becoming the best and highest version of myself. It has required trust, obedience, and perseverance, but the rewards have been immeasurable. I am grateful for the journey, and I look forward to seeing what the future holds.

As we conclude this journey of becoming the best and the highest, we are reminded that this is not a destination, but a continuous process. It is a journey of growth, transformation, and surrender to God's will and purpose. Insisting on being the best and being used for God's highest purposes requires a deep commitment to God and His agenda.

This commitment involves surrendering our lives, plans, and desires to God and trusting in His sovereignty and goodness. It involves recognizing that we are not sufficient in ourselves but that our sufficiency comes from God. It consists in being willing to pay the price of obedience, trust, and surrender, even when it is challenging.

As we journey through life, we will face challenges, obstacles, and setbacks. We will face times of uncertainty, doubt, and fear. But amid these challenges, we must remember that God is always with us, guiding us, protecting us, and empowering us to overcome.

To enjoy the best and highest life, we must be willing to insist on standing out and being used for God's highest purposes. We must be willing to surrender to God's will
and purpose and to trust in His sovereignty and goodness. We must be willing to pay the price of obedience, trust, and surrender, even when it is challenging.

As we conclude this book, we are reminded that the journey of becoming the best and the highest is a lifelong journey. It is a journey that requires patience, perseverance, and persistence. But it is a journey that is worth taking because it leads to a life of purpose, meaning, and fulfillment.

In the words of Psalmist in Psalm 138:8, *"The Lord will fulfill his purpose for me; your steadfast love, O God, endures forever. Do not forsake the work of your hands."* As we journey through life, let us remember that God has a purpose for each of us and that He will fulfill that purpose if we surrender to Him and trust in His goodness.

Let us also remember that insisting on being the best and being used for God's highest purposes requires a deep commitment to God and His agenda. It requires surrendering our lives, our plans, and our desires to God, and trusting in His sovereignty and goodness.

Also, let us commit to insist on standing out, and being used for God's highest purposes. Let us commit to surrender to God's will and purpose, and to trust in His sovereignty and goodness. Let us commit to paying the price of obedience, trust, and surrender, even when it is challenging.

Let us pray:

"Father in the name of Jesus, by Your power and authority, by Your grace and mercy I ask that You work your work, complete Your work in my life, family, life of my children. Complete Your work in my family, my children, and my career. You began a good work in me and will not abandon me, Lord finish Your good work in me of training, raising, purifying, sanctifying, raising, mental transformation, emotional transformation, spiritual transformation, physical enablement, physical transformation, building me, raising me, blessing me, setting me apart for your work and glory, anointing me. Oh Lord finish Your work in my life, family, church, and career. Oh Lord as You do Your work in me, be glorified in me and my career. If you will be ever glorified on this earth let it be in my life, with my life, and through my life in the name of Jesus."

Are You Ready to Stand Out?

It is important to know that the first and best way to truly "Stand Out" is to walk with God. Throughout the Bible, we see numerous examples of great men and women who achieved remarkable things because they walked closely with their God.

When God instructed Noah to build an ark in preparation for a worldwide flood, he didn't hesitate. He trusted God's plan, even when it seemed absurd to those around him (Genesis 6-9). Noah's willingness to stand out from the crowd and follow God's instructions saved not only his own life but also the lives of his family and two of every kind of animal.

Daniel's commitment to his faith is a shining example of what it means to "Stand Out" in a hostile environment. As a Jewish exile in Babylon, Daniel refused to compromise his values, even when faced with the threat of death (Daniel 1-6). His unwavering conviction and trust in God's power of deliverance ultimately led to his promotion to a position of great influence in the kingdom.

Esther's story is a remarkable example of courage and obedience in the face of overwhelming adversity. As a Jewish queen in a foreign land, Esther risked her own life to intercede on behalf of her people, who were facing genocide (Esther 1-10). Her willingness to trust God's plan and stand out from the crowd ultimately saved the lives of thousands of Jews and secured her place in history as a hero of faith.

These three individuals demonstrate that when we walk with God, we can achieve greatness, even in the most challenging circumstances. Their stories inspire us to trust in God's sovereignty and to stand out from the crowd, even when it's difficult or unpopular.

So, if you desire to "Stand Out" in the Kingdom of God, we invite you to take the first step by deciding to follow the Leader – Jesus Christ. The Bible assures us that "if you confess with your mouth that Jesus is Lord and believe in your heart that God raised him from the dead, you will be saved" (Romans 10:9).

By simply believing in your heart and confessing with your mouth the Lordship of Jesus, His death, burial, and resurrection, you will be saved and empowered to stand out in His Kingdom. Will you take this step of faith today and begin your journey to standing out for God's glory?

As the Bible says in Romans 10:9-10, "If you confess with your mouth that Jesus is Lord and believe in your heart that God raised him from the dead, you will be saved."

If you're ready to take this step, pray with me:

"Dear God, I believe that Jesus Christ is the Son of God. I confess that He died for my sins, was buried, and rose again on the third day. I receive Him as my Lord and Savior. Help me to walk with You and stand out for Your glory. Amen."

Congratulations! You've taken the first step towards standing out in the Kingdom of God.

ABOUT THE BOOK

In a world where believers are called to be the light of the world, "Stand Out: Becoming the Best and the Highest" is a powerful and inspiring guide that will challenge readers to re-examine their priorities, values, and goals, and to seek a higher standard of living that is characterized by sacrifice, service, and a deep commitment to advancing God's kingdom.

This book is a comprehensive and practical guide that explores the various sins that hinder believers from becoming the BEST and HIGHEST version of themselves. From the sin of being a hireling instead of a shepherd to the sin of ignoring, neglecting, or avoiding the call to sacrificial living, this book provides a thorough examination of the obstacles that stand in the way of believers who want to live a life that is truly pleasing to God.

Through its eight chapters, "Stand Out: Becoming the Best and the Highest" takes readers on a journey of discovery and transformation, from understanding God's expectation for His people to displaying His splendor as His servants, and overcoming the sins that hinder us, to embracing the call to sacrificial living and divine processes.

The book concludes by emphasizing the importance of coming to Jesus to experience freedom, satisfaction, and the best and highest life that God has planned for us.

Key Takeaways:

• Understand God's expectations for His people and how to display His splendor as His servants.

• Identify and overcome the sins that hinder believers from becoming the best and highest version of themselves.

• Embrace the call to sacrificial living and divine

processes in pursuit of God's purpose and plans for your life.

• Learn how to come to Jesus to experience freedom, satisfaction, and the best and highest life that God has planned for you.

A SPECIAL CALL TO SALVATION & NEW BEGINNINGS FROM DAVID S. PHILEMON

Dear Beloved,
God loves you deeply and has brought you to this moment for a reason. No matter your past, His love and forgiveness are available to you.

The Bible says in John 3:16, "For God so loved the world that He gave His one and only Son, that whoever believes in Him shall not perish but have eternal life." Jesus Christ came to save you, offering you a new life of purpose and peace.

If you're ready to accept Jesus as your Lord and Savior, pray this simple prayer:

The Salvation Prayer

"Heavenly Father, I come to You in the Name of Jesus. I acknowledge that I am a sinner in need of a Savior. I believe that Jesus Christ is Your Son, that He died for my sins, and that You raised Him from the dead. I repent of my sins and turn to You with my

Whole heart. Jesus, I ask You to come into my life. Be my Lord and my Savior. I surrender my life to You. Fill me with Your Holy Spirit, guide me on the path of righteousness, and help me to follow Your script for my life. Thank you, Father, for saving me. In the name of Jesus. Amen."

Welcome to the Family of God!

If you have just prayed this prayer, Congratulations! You are now a child of God, and heaven is rejoicing. Your journey has begun, and we're here to support you as you grow in faith and discover God's unique plans for you.

Next Steps:
• Connect with a Bible-believing church.
• Read the Bible Daily: God's Word is your guide.
• Pray Regularly: Prayer is your lifeline to God.
• Share Your Faith: Don't keep the good news to yourself.

www.ingramcontent.com/pod-product-compliance
Lightning Source LLC
Chambersburg PA
CBHW071857020426
42331CB00010B/2547